Nam Au Go Go

Falling for the Vietnamese Goddess of War

by

John Akins

The Vineyard Press
Port Jefferson, NY

BY THE SAME AUTHOR

On The Way to Khe Sanh

AUTHOR'S NOTE

This is a work of nonfiction based on my memory and Command Chronology reports from Echo Company, 2nd Battalion, First Marine Regiment, First Marine Division and 1st Combined Action Group, III Marine Amphibious Force. Most memories I have seem like they happened yesterday. Yet, there are names of people, names of places and some events that are erased by time, and perhaps by psychological necessity. I have changed the names of two people to protect their anonymity.

ACKNOWLEDGEMENTS

My thanks to John Slattery, Ph.D., former therapist with the Veterans Administration, and to John Bokan, M.D., Puget Sound Division of the Veterans Administration Health Care System, both of whom helped me realize I should and could tell my story. Thanks to Philip Randolf and J. Andrew Rodriguez, writers whose edits made this book a better read. Special thanks to Joan Fiset, who combined her talent as a writer and a therapist to guide me as I tapped my right brain conscious and subconscious to make something good out of something bad.

Cover art includes a stylized rendition of part of a photo, courtesy Hamlyn Publishing Group, London. Photo first appeared in *NAM The Vietnam War Experience 1965-75.*

first edition

Vineyard Press
106 Vineyard Place
Port Jefferson, NY 11777

ISBN: 1-930067-38-0

Xuan Publishing
Nha Trang, Viet Nam

for Cole

Author's Note:

I believe that the closer to the truth, the better the art.
Please feel free to send your comments, questions
or other means through which you connected to my
work via **www.johnakins.net** or **namaugogo@comcast.net.**

The Look in Her Eyes

A sniper kills a Marine.
Our artillery pounds the ville.
A mother holds her shredded baby in her lap.
His head lolls back.

The dream sellers keep their distance and
wave the flag.
Politicians claim the price of freedom
is worth a few lives.
The men who know are never rid of the look
in her eyes.

– John Akins

Introduction

> There are soldiers who, having come to a threshold, cross through it to be wrenched perversely away from themselves.
>
> – after Bruce Weigl and Walter T. Davis

"Take me to the areas of town where the street fighting happened, where they had to fight door to door," I told the former South Vietnamese soldier who offered to take me around on his motorbike. It is Fall 2000 and I'm in Hue City, 32 years after spending 13 months fighting in the Viet Nam War, or American War as the Vietnamese call it.

As I look at the narrow streets that approach the Citadel, the last Vietnamese emperor's walled city within a city, my eye catches bullet-marked masonry, parts of walls that haven't been knocked down for new construction. I feel a stirring in my gut. My brain shifts; it becomes like a reel-to-reel tape deck on rewind and the stop button hints at another realm. My mind fades into a different landscape. Different sounds, different scenes appear when an old reel starts slowly turning in my head.

When I go back to Viet Nam I'm welcomed by its people. I feel a general sense of ease, of belonging. In some places it's a combination of excitement, and longing, and spookiness. In 1968 I was twenty. I began a thirteen-month stay in the northern section of South Viet Nam. Being young and sheltered when I was dropped into the surreal world of combat had a profound effect on me, and that is what this story is about. Going back there launches me into a time of no taboo. It affirms my never-ending strong connection to a war-torn country and its people, who had to endure the devastation a superpower can dump on them, before turning its back on them, dusting off its hands and putting some spin on it. "Peace with honor" or some bullshit. 'Xin loi' ("sorry") about the four million Viet Nam soldiers and civilians killed.

I go back to the place where kids like me spent a little more than a year caught in a quagmire of repugnance and fascination, where dying and killing and just surviving became the meaning of life. We were caught at a time when we were developing a code of values, beliefs, and sense of self. Some initiation into adulthood! I go back to taste the muck and sweet elixir of an incomprehensible slice of life, when death was as routine as a hiccup.

Between winter 2000 and winter 2002 I went back four times. Once, the U.S. customs agent, upon my return to the States, asked me the purpose of my trip. Without thinking, I said, "to look for my soul." I keep going back because, in a way, I never came home.

I knew little about South Viet Nam when I got there as a soldier. After World War II, the Geneva Accords split Viet Nam into two countries at the 17th Parallel. North Viet Nam was communist and South Viet Nam was ruled by various puppet governments, which were dictatorships, really, supported by the U.S. Hue City had once been the imperial capital of all of Viet Nam. It's located midway between Da Nang and Quang Tri, cities on Highway One, which is the main north-south highway along the coast of Viet Nam. It is a few miles up the Perfume River on the north side of Hi Van Pass. The U.S. military arbitrarily divided South Viet Nam into four geographic areas labeled

I, II, III and IV corps. I-Corps, or "Eye" Corps, covered territory from the Demilitarized Zone, or DMZ, the line of demarcation along the 17th parallel and the Ben Hai River between North and South Viet Nam, to an east - west line just north of Duc Pho and Kontumn, which was the beginning of II Corps. The majority of Marines operated in I-Corps, which included various helicopter landing zones, artillery positions and combat bases, such as Con Thien on the coast near the DMZ, and Khe Sanh. Khe Sanh combat base and Hue City were the two worst places to be in 1968.

The Eye Corps area of operation included the cities and towns of Da Nang, Hue, Quang Tri, Phu Bai, Hoi An, Tam Ky, Chu Lai and sections of the Annamitique Mountain Range and surrounding hills, including the Truong Son Mountains north of Con Thien and the Co Roc Mountains west of Khe Sanh. Khe Sanh is located in the northwest corner of Quang Tri Province, 4 miles from the Laotian border and 14 miles south of the DMZ. The hills just south of the DMZ and surrounding the Khe Sanh Valley were the site of brutal fighting from 1966 through 1971. Known as the "the Hill Fights of 1967," historians write of battles for Hill 55, Marble Mountain, the Rock Pile, Hill 1015, Hill 881 North, 881 South, Hill 558 and Hill 861. Holding uninhabited territory had no significance in this war, so they were often fought over more than once.

Now, whenever I'm near Khe Sanh and the mountains surrounding the valley, or if I'm in areas I fought in later near Tam Ky, a dirty little boomtown 60 kilometers south of Da Nang city on Highway One along the coast, I feel the spookiness of a time when living life to the hilt had a strange meaning. Back then it was a daily walk that meandered back and forth across the edge between life and death. Life was simple then, down to the basics – just get another wake up, last through one day and night in a combat area and start another. In the thick of it, luck was a necessity.

When my guide stopped in the old part of Hue City in the fall of 2000, a cloud of smoke wound through my brain and an edginess squeezed through my torso. I felt a fuse burning toward the volatile mix of epinephrine, nonepinephrine and cortisol draining into my awareness. The edge where I had walked through the smoke of war glowed under a pile of buried memories. I was launched back to the eerie, incomprehensible fascination of combat. I'd been assigned to a battalion that went to the other hell hole of Marine area operations in 1968.

But looking back, I knew the Battle of Hue would be a rush. Days of close-quarters street fighting. The kind of high that led me across the threshold to the dark night, to a different world – the underworld – during the last six months of my time in combat. Back to the days of a new addiction – violence.

I've been to Hue City three times since 2000. I'm drawn to it. It was one of the two worst places a Marine infantryman could be during the worst time of the Viet Nam War – Tet 1968. Tet, or An Tet as it is known in Viet Nam, is the celebration of the Lunar New Year and occurs around the 12th of February. It's the major holiday for Viet Nam, like Christmas, New Year's Eve, Mardi Gras, Halloween all rolled into one two-week-long celebration. Before 1968, both sides in the war observed a truce during the week-long celebration. But Tet 1968 was different. The North hit the South with a coordinated attack throughout the entire territory of South Viet Nam, including Saigon, the capital. 84,000 North Vietnamese Communist and Viet Cong revolutionary troops attacked 36 of 44 provincial capitols, 64 of 242 district capitols and 50 hamlets. The American death toll reached more than 1,000. Much of the Vietnamese fighting force was home for the holidays. U.S. military forces were enjoying the down time. The North pulled off a major surprise. Hue City fell to the North Vietnamese Army and Viet Cong. Anyone suspected of loyalty to the South was executed, around 3,000 civilians. Every major U.S. military base was attacked, which meant most major cities and villages came under assault.

At the time Hue was burning, just after the 1968 Tet offensive began, I was on my way to Khe Sanh combat base, a few miles of mountainous jungle and forest northwest of Hue. Now, when I talk to Vietnamese men who are 40 years and older and I tell them I was at Khe Sanh during Tet, they say, "Oh, very bad." Back then, humping the killer hills from the coast to Khe Sanh, getting ambushed, mortared, rocketed, starving for water, I found myself wishing I was at the Battle of Hue City, fighting in a city, for fuck's sake, not this steep, impenetrable forest and jungle in 120-degree heat. Khe Sanh is known for the 77-day siege, for which General Westmoreland and Secretary of Defense Robert S. McNamara were convinced would be the pivotal battle of the Russian- and- Chinese-supported North Vietnamese Army and their sidekicks, the Viet Cong, against U.S. forces and the Army of the Republic of Viet Nam, or ARVNs, the army loyal to the U.S. backed government of South Viet Nam. The fighting was sporadic. NVA artillery and anti-aircraft gun placements were hidden in caves in the mountains.

Divisions of NVA were dug into the hills and more divisions were massing in the mountains. Supposedly they would attack Khe Sanh base in waves. The valley would be the jumping off place for northern troops moving into South Viet Nam.

The indigenous hill people, the Montagnards, fought for our side. Both sides had disrupted their nomadic lifestyle. The NVA used them for forced labor. The Hmong tribesman usually supported the U.S. coalition. According to the U.S. military leadership, the battle of Khe Sanh would be the major offensive. In one decisive show of force, the thorough defeat of the North Vietnamese Army at the hands of the strongest and most advanced military force in the world would squelch efforts by the Communists and Viet Cong to conquer South Viet Nam. It would be the reverse of the Battle of Dien Bien Phu in 1954, in which Vietnamese Viet Minh revolutionaries defeated the elite French paratroopers. After defeat, the French pulled out of Viet Nam and ended their colonial rule. Viet Nam had won its independence after years of French occupation, which first began around 1883.

President Lyndon Johnson did not want another Dien Bien Phu during his reign. I landed in Con Thien, a Marine combat base near the DMZ along the coast of the South China Sea in February 1968, and fell in with a battalion that began the arduous "hump" to reinforce Khe Sanh. The siege of Khe Sanh turned into a series of prolonged skirmishes and hill fights surrounding the Khe Sanh Valley. Then there was the bombardment of the base by NVA artillery hidden in the mountains. During one period of time, Khe Sanh took an average of 700 rounds a month of incoming artillery and rockets. We lived underground like rats. The base looked like an abandoned dump with empty ammo crates lying around, dud-enemy artillery rounds, litter, blown-up bunkers and hulks of crashed choppers and C-130s and Flying Caribou planes along the airstrip. Craters from artillery rounds were everywhere.

As I learned later, the trade-off for fighting in the streets rather than the mountains would have been a bit dicey. Marines took eight to ten casualties a day in Hue during the 27-day battle. I've yet to meet anyone who fought in Hue. Maybe they would have traded places, wondering about their chances in the mountains and the Siege of Khe Sanh.

The 1st and 3rd Marine divisions and Army 1st Cav suffered huge casualties in the hill fights of 1967, which would be the staging area to launch the assault on Khe Sanh. From Khe Sanh it would be easy to control critical cities like Hue and Da Nang and Quang Tri as well as supply routes and avenues of egress to push further south.

To those of us on the ground, the fighting in the hills just seemed a way for the backseat brass to get some ops in their record books. Some of the heaviest casualties of that period of time for both sides happened on hills 881 South, 881 North, 558, 940, 861 and the ravines they overlooked. U.S. troops would take a hill, sustaining many casualties, leave it and then fight for it again when the NVA reclaimed it. But, intell said Khe Sanh was the prize.

A Green Beret encampment supported by South Vietnamese troops six miles west of Khe Sanh on Highway 9 had been attacked by the NVA with Soviet tanks and overrun. Later, after being ambushed, a platoon of 25

Marines lay dead outside the wire of Khe Sanh for a month before the bodies could be retrieved. The hills around Khe Sanh Valley were brutal, steep, covered by jungle so dense you could hardly swing a machete. Marines were to hold the line at Khe Sanh and all along the DMZ. Secretary of Defense McNamara wanted a string of outposts along the DMZ to stop infiltration by North Vietnamese Army troops. Con Thien, my first stop in 1968 was one of them, Khe Sanh further west was another of the string of bases that were to become "McNamara's Line." Most of the North's supplies, material and men came south down the network of trails called the Ho Chi Minh Trail that wound through Laos and Cambodia. We were not supposed to go there or bomb there.

It was the heat and the terrain and the dense forest and jungle that made me wish I was at Hue. We heard reports about Hue during our 110-day hump to reinforce Khe Sanh. Hue was street fighting, trying to drive the NVA and Viet Cong out of the old part of Hue surrounding the Citadel, the former imperial place. It was modeled after the Forbidden City in China.

Working our way to Khe Sanh, I thought street fighting would be better than humping the hills – getting picked apart by snipers and ambushed by the NVA, which seemed to call the shots on when and where to fight – than getting splattered by the rain of incoming artillery and rockets. The NVA would ambush us and melt away. The forest and jungle were so thick it was impossible to catch them on the move. They'd hit and run and disappear into holes, caves and 10-foot high elephant grass. Any clearings were small and deadly. Their bunkers would be intact alongside the lip of 750-pound bomb craters. The caves and fighting holes dug into thick jungle hillsides were invisible. Their big artillery pieces were mounted on rollers in caves in the surrounding mountains just across the DMZ. When the jets came in, they rolled them back in and switched to anti-aircraft guns. In the hills on our side of the DMZ, the ground troops owned the high ground and it was costly to root them out, to assault uphill through thick, unyielding foliage. Foliage isn't even the right word. It was more like layers of live, green chain-link fence interwoven with thick vines or small trees and zig-zagged around big trees for fence posts.

Day after day we fought the brutal terrain, got hit, called in artillery, and I dug in at night. They'd rain in mortars and rockets. The most mind-shattering terror imaginable is a 100-pound, 6-foot-long, 8-inch diamater stick of dynamite wrapped in steel that is screaming out of the sky on an arc dead-center into your foxhole. There is no sweating, crying or shitting your pants. All systems are shut down, overridden by stark, cerebral terror.

It seemed hopeless, suicidal. You had to go into the caves you were assaulting like White and Miller did, two savvy guys who knew how to react and how to survive. As an FNG, (Fucking New Guy), I watched them closely.

I've talked to other Marines who were humping to Khe Sanh in 1968 and were hoping for a bullet, whether a "million-dollar wound," the kind that got you home but not too fucked-up - a wrist or ankle joint, a bit of ligament or tendon smashed by shrapnel or a bullet to get you out of the war, to end the agony of 60-to-70-pound packs and a radio or machine gun and ammo for the machine gun, plus their own rifles, ammo, grenades, claymores and so on, along with three canteens of water.

At that time, I would have taken street fighting in Hue in a heartbeat. But years later, I think not about the brutal terrain and daily rain of artillery I would have skated, I think about the action – door-to-door street fighting – yeah, lots of action. Lots of contact, right in the neighborhood. Between Tet and the 13 months that followed, my outlook changed – the revulsive taste of war sweetened. The change was incremental. Forget a million-dollar wound. I got hooked, got bent.

A 27-day battle in the streets would have been an addict's greatest score. As it turned out, Khe Sanh folded around June 1968. While we cleaned up the debris and blew bunkers, I was transferred to small team units called Combined Action Platoons – a few Marines, a corpsman and a squad of South Vietnamese troops. CAPs set up compounds near villages or collections of hamlets to defend them against NVA and Viet Cong aggression and to provide some civic action assistance.

The mission was twofold – clear out the enemy and win the hearts and minds of the civilians. The word was that CAPs got overrun all the time. Some did. During one period of a few years, 800 of 1,500 CAP Marines were killed. Lots of action, up close guerrilla fighting – small numbers and deadly.

Still today, I have many stories, fragments of the whole experience. Each fragment is a piece of shrapnel in my mind that I try to dig out.

Chapter One
I Go In

There was something odd about the quiet Native American instructor in the Infantry Training Regiment at Camp Pendelton in early 1968. He wasn't a loud, hard-charger Marine like the other instructors. He never said anything, even to the other instructors. He followed behind the platoon on 2-hour marches to various classes with the downcast look of a hollow man. He seemed the ultimate loner – spiritually dead. I guessed he'd been to Viet Nam. He never said so, but you could see it in his blank eyes. It was as if he'd seen too much, done too much. In fact, he was the only instructor of our training company who had been in combat. Thirteen months later, I would know what made him so different.

The military was something on my "To Do" list: After college, do the military thing and then get a career and family. No big thing. In fact, there were a couple more flippant reasons for joining the Marines in 1967. I didn't know what I was doing in college, and MaryRae, my first true love, seemed to lose interest in me. It was the spring of my sophomore year. I just wasn't moving fast enough in all directions. She probably picked up on the fact that I didn't know where I was going. I changed my course of study every quarter depending on my grades. I never thought about marriage. That was pretty far down on the list.

"We're too young. You shouldn't get married till you get out of college and have a good job," I'd advise.

"My parents got married when my mom was sixteen," she'd counter.

I found out the bad news from her younger brother.

"MaryRae's seeing someone else. A guy who just got out of the Navy."

Toward the end of spring I had to register for fall quarter. Spring quarter sophomores had to declare a major, and I had no idea what to do. I was also one credit behind the required total to maintain a 2-S student draft deferment, which meant I was eligible for the draft. It was 1967. I would have to enroll in summer quarter. I signed up for a class, but I never went. I got a great job working on an underground water line out in the boonies, around Duvall, Washington, a 40-minute drive from Seattle. The old barrel slats and iron-ring-bound water pipeline was being replaced by a 52-inch diameter metal pipe. It ran for miles underground, including under the Tolt River.

Mornings were bright and crisp and the pipe was dark and cool. Real quiet. Hatches were cut every quarter mile where the pipe ran above ground on stanchions. Big fans kept air moving through the pipe, which blew the toxic smoke from the tar we used to seal joints and patch gouges in the special surface coating the inside of the pipe. You could barely make out the faint hum of a fan blowing fresh air somewhere down the line.

After work, I went to my room in a boarding house that was being remodeled. Some mornings the ceiling would fall in as I brushed my teeth. But I had free rent at the Jean-Paul Sarte No Exit Memorial Rooming House and Alice's Rèstaurant, and the landlord, an associate professor at the University of Washington, sold me marijuana for $15 a lid. I noticed this blonde sitting on the porch across the street when I parked my car after work. It seemed like she was always there. One afternoon I went over to introduce myself and found out she dug the dirty-T-shirt construction look – so I never went to class. Linda Lakin from Havertown, Philadelphia would give me hope at times during my tour in the jungle.

I'd never talked to anybody who was in the service. I'd heard that a couple high school classmates had gone in and one had supposedly gotten killed over there.

The Marine Corps had a two-year volunteer enlistment program in 1967, which was an exception due to the need for warm bodies. You could delay entry into boot camp for 120 days. I knew that draftees were usually the only guys who could do the minimum two years of active duty. Volunteers into any branch had to do a least three years, usually four for the Navy or Air force. This was my summer of big bucks and the timing would allow me to earn a pile of money.

I was walking down University Avenue near the University of Washington and passed the Navy and Marine Corps recruiting office. The Navy Seabees, the construction battalion, had a waiting list and it was three years of duty anyway.

I turned to the Marine recruiter:

"If I volunteer, would I get to choose what kind of assignment I would have?"

"Right. If you get drafted into the army, they'll just put you in infantry and ship you to Viet Nam."

He just didn't tell me when I'd get to choose. He showed me the list of military occupations. Clerical stuff, supply stuff, transportation stuff, communications stuff. I was naive. I signed a contract. About the time fall quarter started in 1967, I went to the Marine Corps Recruit Depot in San Diego. Boot camp. I never got to ask about assignments. You answered questions, never asked any. I got permission to ask a question the day before we graduated. I waited 12 weeks for the burning question:

"When do I get to choose what my assignment will be?"

"Don't worry about it, Akins. You already have orders for WESTPAC, Western Pacific. You're infantry, 0311 – rifleman. You're going to Nam Au' Go Go, where the action is."

The physical part of boot camp was right up my alley, and the harassment part by. the drill instructors was downright hilarious at times. Scary at others. I'd already been through a fraternity initiation hell week where upperclassman haze you in shifts 24 hours a day for a week. I guess the whole idea was based on military boot camp. It felt familiar. Our drill instructors, though, wanted perfection.

This one guy had a bad complexion. The Drill Instructor shouted:

"YOU FUCKING SCUMBAG. WHY ARE THERE ZITS ALL OVER YOUR FACE? YOU BETTER FUCKING GET RID OF THAT CRUD OR I'LL DIG THEM OUT WITH MY BALLPOINT PEN. WHY ARE YOU IN MY PLATOON YOU PIZZA-FACED ASSHOLE!"

The DI was inches from the kid's face waving the ink tube from a ball-point pen in his face.

The badasses from back on the block in Chi town and New York were in for a surprise. They would end up begging to be released, crying for their mothers. Not only did you rarely speak, except to scream to answer a question, but back talk didn't cut it. The mouthy ones ended up in Correctional Custody if they weren't hospitalized, or in Motivation Platoon where they spent 10 hours a day filling buckets of sand and carrying them across the base to make a big sand pile. They carried them on the end of poles across the shoulders just like the shoulder poles Vietnamese peasants used. Then they had to start boot camp all over again. The thought of being recycled through boot camp was enough to motivate most guys. But there may have been some enlightened ones who tried to make a career out of boot camp to avoid the Nam.

"WHY ARE YOU EYE-FUCKING ME YOU FUCKING SCUMBAG. ARE YOU IN LOVE WITH ME SHIT-FOR-BRAINS? WHERE THE FUCK ARE YOU FROM? ARE YOU FROM CALIFORNIA? YOU FAGGOT. WHAT ARE YOU DOING IN MY GODDAM PLATOON? ARE YOU TRYING TO FUCK UP MY MARINE CORPS? GIVE ME SQUAT THRUSTS FOR EVER AND EVER YOU FUCKING FAIRY."

They pretty much kept us isolated from the rest of the world. No news, no music, no connection with the outside. They discouraged mail.

"ALL YOU SWINGING DICKS MAY AS WELL FORGET ABOUT MARY-ROTTEN-CROTCH BACK HOME. SHE IS TOO BUSY FUCKING YOUR FRIENDS, COUSINS AND BROTHERS. AND IF ANY OF YOU ASSHOLES WRITE YOUR CONGRESSMAN I WILL FUCKING RIP YOUR HEAD OFF AND SHIT DOWN YOUR NECK."

Sundays was mail call. You stood in formation. When they called your name you sprinted to the front, stood at attention with your arms extended, palms touching and hands spread wide in a vertical position. The letter was inserted into the jaws of the trap and you snapped down on it and scurried off.

I'd always been pretty high-spirited when it came to running – usually chasing a ball or someone carrying one, or any challenge of physical strength. During the early 1960s, John Kennedy said American youth were weak and instituted a fitness improvement program in the public school system. I went for it.

The drill marching on the parade ground was cool, too. There is something about 40 men moving precisely in formation turning square corners, every command executed in perfect unison. The rhythm of every footstep making a single thud on a marching cadence becomes a little hypnotic. A Marine platoon is lined up tall to short, front to back. Four of us little guys marched abreast as the last rank and were unable to see anything going on in front of us. I am naturally curious, which occasionally got me in trouble.

"AKINS. FUCKING WORTHLESS PIECE-OF SHIT-COLLEGE-DROP-OUT. ARE YOU EYE FUCKING THE AREA? FALL OUT AND GIVE ME SQUAT THRUSTS FOR EVER AND EVER. READY BEGIN."

Squat, thrust your legs back, do a push-up, snap your legs under you and jump up. I did a session of squat thrusts in the sand once and had a trench dug about 20 inches deep after half an hour.

After boot camp, Infantry Training Regiment was a little looser. You could talk when you weren't busy in a class. We did two-hour forced runs with full gear to classes every day and tried not to panic in the tear gas hut. We had to keep calm because there were a couple of instructors with masks on and if anybody put their mask on too soon the instructors would tear the mask off and sit on the guy until they figured he'd been reminded to obey orders. They had the doors barricaded from the outside, so there was no crashing the doors, although some tried.

What's bad is that you were going through the final couple of weeks of training with about a hundred or so freshly brainwashed "John Waynes" who were eager to try out their new manhood. A few went to Oceanside, California on weekend liberty and got their asses kicked by some tired-of-the-bullshit civilians. The small guys were constantly getting challenged. That's where I learned how to fight. Pick up a board, a rock or something. I liked a broom. These Hollywood types couldn't wait to go into battle and become heroes. During training I learned from a Newsweek article that Marine infantry was taking 80 percent casualties. When I pointed this out to one annoying dumbshit, he wanted to fight.

"WHAT ARE YOU, A COMMUNIST?" he said. He started swinging. He was black, so our little rumble lit off a mini race riot. The MPs went crazy swinging their clubs.

I made a couple of friends in boot camp, Harold and Guy. They weren't brainwashed, and they weren't bohunks or crackers or thugs who made a choice between a prison sentence and the Marine Corps. Each had at least a year of college. You really can't get to know someone until ITR, where you can open your mouth. So there's opportunity to visit, talk about home, why you ended up in the service. Guy was from Astoria, a small town on the coast of Oregon. He had that kind of checklist reason for going into the military.

"Well, I figured I had to do the service thing and I'd get drafted anyway. So I figured I go in, get it out of the way.

"It will look good on our resumes."

"And if I got sent to Nam, I'd find out what's really going on."

Harold was from the Midwest. A typical straight shooter and unassuming guy. We had one encounter that I thought was odd. One morning we both ended up at the latrine at the same time. I was headed for a stall and he suggested we sit in adjacent stalls so we could chat. It seemed odd. I didn't think of this kind of function as relaxation. Anyway, we chatted. We went together on the one weekend pass toward the end of ITR. We got a motel room and a fifth of whiskey and spent a quiet weekend reading newspapers and going to movies. We weren't going to waste time being Marine icons trying to pick up local muff. We pretty much knew what a waste of energy that was.

When we got overseas, Guy and I got assigned to different infantry battalions and Harold got assigned to Military Police. He was standing in line in front of me when he got MPs. That seemed like safer duty than infantry, so when it came to my turn, I volunteer for MPs. No deal.

"Well, I can type. I can type." For the first couple months, I kept telling my superiors I could type. Every grunt's dream was to get a job at a rear base camp once they learned the bush was a deadly motherfucker. I never could get one. As I got deeper into my tour, I didn't want one.

During my tour, I got dysentery and was in the rear area, probably Phu Bai, for treatment. I spent a lot of time in the latrine. Once, while in there, certain I would not have any digestive tract left, I picked up a Stars and Stripes, the military newspaper. It published a list of weekly casualties. That's where I learned Harold was dead.

I didn't know what happened to Guy Yancy until after the end of my tour in Nam, when I ran into him at the transition barracks on Treasure Island Naval Base.

Once, during a lull in some training exercise at ITR, I approached the forlorn-looking Native American instructor.

"You were over there, right?"

He nodded affirmatively.

"So, what do you think?"

"Most of you are gonna be killed."

I became a replacement in Echo Company, Second Battalion, First Marine Regiment, First Marine Division. They were operating in the Mountains near the Demilitarized Zone. Midway through the month-long 1968 Tet Offensive I was humping the hills on the way to reinforce Khe Sanh Combat Base.

Chapter Two
Humping to Khe Sanh

A sense of foreboding blocked out every feeling I could have felt. That's all I can remember about arriving in Viet Nam. I don't remember the smell. I don't remember the heat. I remember a sense of doom.

The Boeing 707 taxied to a stop at the Da Nang airfield. I looked out the small window on board and let out a deep sigh. The thought is still vivid. Thirteen months to go. I wonder if I'll make it.

I rode with other replacements in the back of a deuce-and-a-half truck past an area called Dogpatch. There were the shanties, walls of woven reeds or flattened beer cans and boards from freight pallets. Crowded and smoky and alive with hawkers. Especially kids, all asking for money, candy or cigarettes. Packed and teeming.

Shacks and hovels lined both sides of the dirt road. Motorbikes and bicycles were heaped high with cargo. That's what I remember about Dogpatch. I didn't see the teenage working girls, the hookers. At the staging area, a series of large tents with wooden floors, I immediately got conned by some guys who were on their way back to the world, as the states were referred to.

"Hey I'll sell you these jungle utilities (fatigues) for five bucks. There's a shortage of them and you'll cook to death in those stateside utilities."

"Okay."

My next stop was the supply tent where I picked up a complete set of jungle utilities. Hmmm... But, I didn't get jungle boots, which caused me much extra exertion as I slipped and slid and stumbled up and down trails, wearing stateside boots with flat soles. I got a helmet, flak jacket, M-16 rifle and backpack with poncho and poncho liner. The next day, I went to assignment processing where cold-hearted clerks turned me down for clerk, supply and even MP jobs.

"Be at the flight line tomorrow at 0700. A chopper will take you to your infantry company, Echo Company, Second Battalion out of Con Thien fire base. They need all the replacements they can get."

"Hey. I can type. Are you sure there aren't any clerk openings?"

The chopper ride was my first look at Viet Nam countryside and it was beautiful. Nicely laid out squares of water surrounded by dikes that later would become emerald patches of growing rice. Collections of brown thatched huts were sprinkled under palm trees. The air was so clean. The shades of green were such a contrast to the blue sky.

We flew over the beach along the South China Sea north to Phu Bai. The sand looked like a soft white blanket smoothly tucked between the edge of the dense brush line and the edge of the blue-green surf. Phu Bai had a Marine fire base not far off of Highway One, the main north-south road that stretched along the whole country. Up north, parts of Highway One were also called the The Street Without Joy. I remember nothing about Phu Bai. I spent the night in a tent with cots, the last time I would sleep on anything but the ground until I got wounded.

The next day, another chopper dropped six of us Fucking New Guys at the Con Thien firebase. It was a little rise in the denuded area near the DMZ where bunkers and trenches had been dug into the red dirt. The ground had been so bombarded by air strikes and artillery that there were just patches of vegetation left. The base looked like a garbage dump. You couldn't stay above ground long enough to police the area. Continual incoming. It was overcast, the brush in the surrounding hills looked almost blue. In the compound, everything but the artillery pieces was below ground or two-thirds below and surrounded by walls of sandbags. We stood in front of the command bunker, where three squad leaders eyed us warily. I really had no clue where we were. Every place was just a name. I'd never seen a map of Viet Nam.

"Gentlemen," Echo Cómpany's lanky captain greeted us. "About three klicks out there is the DMZ, the line that separates North and South Viet Nam. Those are the Co Roc Mountains, where there are backup NVA and their artillery sites. Making contact with the enemy is just like a football game. After that first hit, you're over the jitters. Panko, take these guys to get haircuts and then divide them up between the three squads."

I couldn't believe he was worried about haircuts. And comparing combat to football? I figured him for a real screwball.

The next day was my first day in the bush. A platoon-sized patrol went outside the wire toward the mountains. The ground was red dirt. The scrub brush was low and thinned out. It was hot, very hot. I was given an extra two boxes of M-60 machine gun ammo that were tied together in a sling to carry for the machine gunner. After a couple hours humping through country that reminded me of sagebrush desert in Eastern Washington, except the brush was deep green, I was beat. I felt so hot my face seemed on fire and the gun ammo, slung across my shoulders and banging my hips, got real heavy. We paused at an NVA corpse that was still smoking from a gun ship rocket that hit close enough to shred his back. He was laying face down and I was surprised at how big he was – more than six feet. One of the new guys, a black guy, drilled the corpse with a full burst of his M-16. He stood with his feet spread and his chest puffed out, but with a weird look on his face. A John Wayne, I figured, couldn't wait to pull the trigger. But shooting at a dead body seemed very weird.

On the way back, I was struggling with the gun ammo. The heat was beating me up. I figured I shouldn't have to carry the extra ammo the whole day so I left it on the trail for someone else to pick up.

"Never leave ammo on the trail like that," my squad leader said.

"With all these guys, why should I have to carry the extra weight all day?"

I think the haircut and the pep talk had already made me start questioning the judgment of my leaders. We stopped again at the now thoroughly dead corpse.

"Hey bro, gimme some water," another Marine said.

I did.

Back in the wire one of the Marines told me that everyone was supposed to carry water and not to give mine away.

"You never know how long it will have to last and how long it will be before we come across more."

It surprised me that someone would bother to give a new guy advice. You were pretty much persona non grata until you'd proven yourself when the shit hit the fan.

That night I had my first taste of contact while standing watch in a trench along the perimeter of the base. I was handed the radio and stood peering into the shadows. I don't know how far away the next Marine was and had no idea what to expect or how I would react if I saw something.

"Charlie Three this is Echo 6. Gimme a sid rep over." The radio "shhhed" a little static then went quiet. Then the voice returned.

"Charlie three this is Echo 6. Sip rep, over."

I keyed the handset.

"What?" I forgot to say "over."

"Three this is Echo six. What's your situation report, over?"

I keyed the hand set. "This is Echo Three, uhh, nothing happening, over."

"When I call you, just say 'all secure negative contact.' Echo 6 out."

"Ah, what?"

The radio spit and shhhed. "Three this is Echo Six. Just say 'all secure, negative contact' Six out."

My first lesson in radio watch..

I cringed when I suddenly saw a pair of eyes that quickly disappeared. I strained looking into the night. Others appeared and disappeared 30 meters in front of me. They were in the wire. I ducked and peered just over the edge of the trench. Pairs of eyes were appearing and disappearing. I was sweating. But they were green. Relieved, I figured I just witnessed fire flies for the first time. The way they seemed to flit around in pairs was unnerving. I continued to carefully watch the fireflies to be certain it wasn't some sort of devilish trick. Suddenly, I heard a pop and a figure came running down the trench at me. I jumped out of the trench and pointed my M-16. Then I heard a voice in English.

"Help. I'm hurt."

It was the guy who asked me for water earlier. He was doubled over holding his hand which had a sizable hole through the palm. He shot himself with a 45 caliber pistol.

A few days later I was called into the command bunker to answer questions about the incident. The guy had been charged with committing a self-inflicted wound. It was a way out of the bush, out of the war and out of the Marine Corps. Months later, one of the guys in the squad got a boastful letter from him while he was in the hospital in Tokyo. He was getting a medical discharge. I wondered how his hand turned out. Later, the idea of self-inflicted wound crossed my mind.

My company left Con Thien on about a 90-day operation to hump to Khe Sanh firebase to reinforce it for the siege. Khe Sanh was in a valley surrounded by the Truong Son and Co Roc mountains where the NVA was heavily dug in. This hump turned into the most brutal physical test I would ever encounter. The hills were so steep and jungle so dense it sometimes took five hours to go a couple of kilometers. Temperatures got to 120 degrees.

"You haven't been in country long have you? You're pretty pale. Better make sure you carry plenty of water."

I was sitting alongside a trail, stupefied. The hardest physical strain I'd ever encountered was humping those hills for months. Hour after hour, then digging in at night. I had to tear up thick, green grass carpet before I could dig three or four feet into the ground. Then you stood watch every two or three hours. Climb up and down and hack through the forest for 10 hours and dig in.

When we think of combat we think about fear and killing, not about slowly being ground to death by the sheer strain of living mobile. You hump a heavy load – a pack, ammo, a weapon and perhaps the radio. Infantrymen walk. Up mountains, through rivers. There is very little flat land around the DMZ. This is mountainous, dense jungle. The climbs are steep and you fight the bush every step of the way, unless you're half way back in the column. By then there's a bit of a beaten path. It's 110 degrees. You carry your water – three canteens. You don't know when you'll come across water again. It could be a stream or a bomb crater filled with rainwater. One time, a chopper brings in a large bladder filled with water on a sling. It can't land on the side of the hill so it hovers over a clearing as low as it can go. It drops the load and we watch in amazement as it bounces and crashes through the jungle down the hillside. It's an easy walk to and from the bladder. It cleared some jungle flat.

The column snakes through waist-high elephant grass interspersed with clumps of trees and bamboo. It's morning, so the heat doesn't quite bake us into a pained stupor. Knowing that we will be humping for 10 hours puts me into sort of a pained trance. Suddenly, the rrrrrowwww of AK-47 rounds roars through the brush ahead of me and Randy, my team leader. We dive into a huge bomb crater and crawl to the lip. Peeking out, Randy says we better watch to the rear. I could have hugged him. The shooting for the most part remains further up the line.

Moments later his hand flinches. A quarter-inch piece of shrapnel from a mortar round rolled up and rested against the back of his hand. It's hot and leaves a little red mark. He picks up the piece and studies it.

"Hey, maybe you should put me in for a purple heart."

During a firefight one afternoon, Miller and White blaze away at an opening in the hillside then duck in and bring out two NVA soldiers. Miller and White are in my platoon, different squad. They each have five or six months in country, which seems like a lifetime to me. I feel gloomy whenever I think of how much time I have left on my tour. They are bold, aggressive soldiers and know how to react when the shit hits the fan. I'm in awe of their courage and covet their survival skills. I watch them closely.

A few minutes later we are on our way again. When we stop moving to let others catch up, or to let the lieutenant to check the map, I sit at the side of the trail. My head hanging, I feel like the movie images of a guy frying in the Sahara Desert. The sun is so bright and the insulating effect of eight-foot tall elephant grass, bamboo and other jungle shrub intensifies the heat.

Being a new guy, I walk point much of the time. I'm an unknown quantity, not tight with anybody, so I'm expendable. Walking point not only means being the first guy into an ambush or a sniper's sights, but having to hack an opening through the heavy curtain of jungle.

In Seattle, 70 degrees is a hot day. I strain up hills, but it's like trying to pull myself from the bottom of a deep pool with hip waders on. My pack, ammo and weapon total 60-plus pounds. I weigh 125. I launch myself against the growth as if breaking down a door. I hope no one hears me. I'm surrounded by greenery – the elephant grass, the razor grass, the bamboo, the trees, vines and stuff. My gear pushes on my neck, drags on my legs as I climb in the killing heat. Sometimes we are under white baking sky. Sometimes we hump under triple canopy jungle like walking through a sticky industrial oven. The arms and back of my shirt stiffen and turn white from the dried salt that oozes from my body. A crease at the elbow rubs my skin raw.

We make it to the top of a hill a couple of hours after nightfall. Our four-man team is too beat to dig in. We lay our ponchos on the ground and lay side by side about 20 meters from a tree line.

Someone shakes me awake.

"Come on. We've got to move out."

I notice shadows moving about. The corpsman is on my right, kneeling at Rodriguez's feet. He's been hit by a grenade, the same one that killed Baker who lay next to me. I've slept through a grenade attack.

We make it to a valley at the foot of the Truong Suong and Co Roc mountains. We provide perimeter security while preparations are made to build an LZ, a landing zone for choppers. The site is called Ca Lu. We work at stringing a single strand of barbwire around the perimeter. We dig in among some 500-gallon bladders of JP jet fuel. We guard the fuel.

"Is this stuff flammable?"

"No. It can take a direct hit and not blow."

Of course, later I learn it is moderately flammable. The word is that we will head to Hill 881 South. The NVA are dug in. The hill fights for 881 North and 881 South along with 558, 861, 940 and 689 had cost a lot of lives. Marines fought for months and took heavy casualties. Then they left. Now we are going to take them back. We need these positions to protect Khe Sanh base in the valley below. The hills are a buffer between Khe Sanh Plain and the mountains where NVA troops are massing for the big battle of Khe Sanh. I have a vague idea these hills are near the DMZ.

The word that the hills surrounding Ca Lu are crawling with NVA deflates many Marines' John Wayne images. They see death all around, not opportunities for heroism. The reality of combat and fear of dying replaces the Hollywood image of war and heroism so many bought into.

One morning my squad leader kicks the sole of my boot to wake me up. Anger flashes in my head and I pick up my rifle.

"Don't ever wake me up like that again, asshole."

"Just get ready to go on patrol."

I just didn't like the guy. His nasal voice and southern accent grated on me. He seemed nervous all the time, which set me on edge.

I liked Randy, my team leader, though. Ever since that first contact when we stayed back instead of moving toward the enemy fire, I thought he was okay. We were pounding in steel fence stakes one day on the perimeter at Ca Lu when he got the idea that if I pushed him off the 55-gallon drum he was standing on to drive in the stake, he might break his arm and get out of the bush. I pushed the barrel over and he tumbled into the knee-high thick grass.

"Try it again."

The landing was too soft.

"I can break your elbow for you," I promised. "All I have to do is twist your arm and hit the back of your elbow. It only takes about seven pounds of force. That's nothing."

"Nah, just push me off one more time."

I get a little tight with Mervyn, a black dude in my team. He faithfully writes his girl friend Rose every day. This dream of his, this bond he has or thinks he has, is a refreshing sentiment. He must've wondered about the macho thing one day. I'm sitting on some sandbags alongside a fuel bladder when he jumps me. I roll him off me and get him in a choke hold.

"Okay," I said. "I give up."

I let him save face and let it go at that. He sticks up for me when we finally get to Khe Sanh. My aloofness, my unwillingness to play cards or engage in the constant one-upmanship banter, probably didn't sit well with the rest of the platoon. When I got garbage detail for about the fifth day in a row up in Khe Sanh, Mervyn told our squad leader to fuck off, to "quit dumping the shit on my man Akins."

One day we were sitting watching A-4s and Phantoms working out over the trees near our position at Ca Lu. The 500-pound and 250-pound bombs shook the ground and smoked up the sky. On some runs they dropped napalm and you'd get a peek occasionally of a streak of orange fire. It was comforting. We would be humping those hills, making our way to Khe Sanh.

The scout-dog handler was not comforted. He stopped by our position during one of the air shows.

"Intelligence says there's two regiments of NVA in those hills. We're going in there tomorrow or the next day."

The dog was a beautiful animal. I thought about how nice it would be to have a keen pair of ears and sensitive nose with you in the bush. A buddy who would never annoy you, only love you.

"You know I go wherever this dog goes," said the handler. "So if he gets sick, wounded or killed, I get medevaced with him. A little rat poison and I'm out of here."

He was medevaced before we left Ca Lu.

The company poked its head into the bush and started climbing. I walked point. Even if our squad was somewhere down the line, the word came down. "Akins up." The easy days guarding "nonflammable" jet fuel were over. The mule team moved out. After getting to the top of a ridge line, the terrain opened up. Clumps of trees and bamboo broke up the waist-high elephant grass. I came across a narrow trail and followed it. I passed bomb craters that were four- or five-foot deep pockets of freshly turned over red dirt. The smaller ones carved out by 250-pound high explosive bombs, were about six feet across. The inverted red cones left by 500-pound bombs were impressive.

I had about 10 days in country and had that new guy caution. My senses were keyed up. I hadn't picked up that herd mentality, just plodding along wishing for cooler weather and lighter loads. If I followed a trail, one that hadn't been worn into a dirt path, I went slow. I strained to hear any sound, watched for any brush that moved.

I was still an outsider, which was not a good thing. Who knows if someone will crawl up and drag you back or give a shit if you get hit? Yet, I didn't really care. I didn't like 95 percent of the guys that made up this platoon. I wasn't an elitist or intolerant, but I really had no way of connecting with them. Some acted so stupid. I think I resented being with them. Later, things would change. The only guy I could talk to was the Navy corpsman, who had more to say than "jive talk'n" disrespect about my mother.

One day coming back from taking a piss a ways off from the column, I find myself surrounded by three black guys from back on the block, Chi town or Detroit, maybe.

"The brother here is going on R&R and needs some money. Give him some money."

"No can do man," I shrug.

"Man, you haven't been around long enough to spend any money. We know you got money, so give some to the brother."

I look around and there is no one in sight. I figure getting loud wouldn't draw much attention, so I reach into my pocket and pull out some bills. The only time I've ever been mugged, I'm in the jungle during a war.

As we climb and dig in day after day, I start to like point. When the shit hits, I can usually tell where it's coming from, which makes things less hairy. But hacking through a solid wall of brush towering over my head is hell. There'd be no trail and swinging a machete in 110 degrees is a killer. One day the bamboo and elephant grass is so tall and thick, it just swallows me. I can't even swing a machete. I use my body like a battering ram.

"Here carry this. I can't even swing it."

I stick it in the ground for a big black guy, a new guy I've never seen before. As I turn to continue ramming the jungle, he kicks me in the back. I get up and level my M-16 at him. I'm thinking fast. Fire a burst into this asshole and then just start shooting ahead wildly. Just as I'm about to fire a burst, a boot 2nd Lieutenant comes around the bend.

"What's going on?"

I've never seen an officer this close to the point

element.

"Hey, lieutenant, want to lead the way?"

We got part way up a steep slope by about 9 pm. Our squad leader told us to spread out and watch down the hill. We'd have watch every two hours. I was just below the ridge line hanging on to a tree that curved out from the bank. It started out of the ground horizontal and then curved up vertical. The only way I could stay on the slope was to straddle the trunk and lean back against the hill. No sleep that night, but I didn't have to dig in.

The next morning the column clanks along, as usual, in the thick green oven. Squad leaders holler to each other.

"Are you guys on our right flank? Move up."

I cringe at all the racket. Aren't they worried about where the enemy is? I thought the idea was to move quietly. How did guys last very long in infantry against an enemy that owns these forests? The climb levels out as the forest gives way to an opening flanked by tree lines.

We are hugging one of the tree lines when the afternoon erupts into a cacophony of staccato automatic fire and screams all around. This is how it always starts – a blazing eruption of fire and confusion. You never know the exact location of the firing unless you were point. I duck against a tree trunk facing the opposite tree line. Something flashes about four feet over my head and shears the tree into a rain of splinters. A rocket had been fired at me. Finally I snap to and start firing wildly into the tree line. Minutes into the fight, a chopper shows up. It swoops into the downside of the slope, the door gunners sweeping the area. It hovers an instant about six feet off the ground, and two FNGs join our outfit in the middle of a firefight. They freeze an instant and run into the closest tree line.

They have the biggest wide-eyed, shocked looks I've ever seen.

No one caught sight of any of the NVA that hit us. No one could guess the size of the element. The shooting stopped and we swept the tree line. We didn't find a trace of them. We didn't find a bunker, a hole, nothing. All we knew was that they had been pretty much on top of us. I looked at the tree I'd been under. It was a six-inch diameter pole all splintered at the end. The rest of it had been blown back four feet.

"That was an RPG. Rocket-propelled grenade, dude," Randy said.

"They use those on tanks and bunkers."

Jets were working out as we moved out. We were heading to another hill where we could hack out an LZ and set up a perimeter. From there we would get a lift to our next destination, an assault on Hill 558.

The hump was more of the same bone-weary plodding in the blazing heat. The sun turned into a prism that focused steel-cutting rays through my helmet to fry my brain. My flak jacket was stiff insulation wrapped in squares of fiberglass that banged and rubbed at my waist. My pants sagged from the grenades and cans of C- rations in the side pockets. The 60-pound pack was another layer on the convection oven we wore to cook us dry. I carried the barest infantry issue: A poncho and poncho liner, two to three days of C-rations, some extra M-16 magazines, a fold-up shovel. There were no extra socks or underwear. We didn't wear underwear or socks. The socks would rot and the underwear was an extra layer of clothing to incubate heat rash. The rest of the pack stored extra fragmentation grenades and smoke grenades and battle dressings.

On my belt I carried more frag grenades and three canteens of water and a gas mask. I threw the mask away and carried a paperback in the pouch. Every time we stopped on a trail I broke out the paperback. I thought reading would keep me from going brain-dead.

I wondered if the two new guys had their wits about them yet. What a way to join an outfit – they probably just hit the deck and stayed put. At least they didn't get the bullshit pep talk. But their fear factor must be at an all-time high. Being a new guy isn't just being clueless. No one gives a shit about you. No one would bat an eye if you got blown away.

It takes time to be accepted by your squad members. If you're lucky someone will take the initiative to speak to you, maybe even tell you where the hell you are if they have any idea. Most of the time you just follow the guy ahead of you not knowing where you are and wondering when your number will be up. It seems weird, but you've got more on your mind, like how am I going to make it 13 months. At first, when the shit hits, you get down and stay down. No one tells you what to do. They are reacting. Fire at the sound of automatic weapons and move. Move at the fire. It's a strange concept to adopt. But gradually fear is replaced by reaction. Drop, fire, move toward the shooting.

I'm afraid I'll go crazy or that my mind will go dim. I'll become this mindless grunt like those all around me. I'm still an outsider. Crawling up and dragging my wounded squad leader back under fire doesn't earn me entrance into the club. They probably read me like a book – I think they're crackers or hoods. Stupid.

Day after day, I'm at the front of the column. "Akins up." It happens about 20 or 30 minutes after we move out. I walk past everybody as they sit. The blacks wipe their faces with the green towels they keep draped around their necks. Everyone keeps a clear plastic bottle of insect repellent in a rubber band around their helmet. Some keep a battle dressing or two there. They're about the size of a pack of cigarettes, a little thicker, in a brown package.

The dressing itself is a thick pad with long tails for binding and tying. We've all been taught to use the cellophane off a pack of cigarettes to seal off a sucking chest wound. You know their lung is hit because the blood from the wound is frothy with bubbles and the wound is gurgling. I have my blood type, "B-pos" in thick block letters on the back of my flack jacket.

There's really not that much cellophane available in a company because there's not that many packs of cigarettes available. Everybody shares cigarettes, candy, letters from home. Smokes and candy come in extra supplies called SPs – special somethings. It's a regular-sized cardboard box full of packs of cigarettes and candy. They came every once in a while on a supply chopper. It was a special day whenever I happened to be close enough when one was broken into to get a slim pack of those jellied candies that are sugar coated. I'd strike for the candy and then stand back during the fight over Salems and Marlboros. When the squabbling subsided, I took what was left—unfiltered Pall Malls. A few red packages were always there at the bottom of the box or tossed aside. These smokes were rolled and shipped that year. C-rations had a little box of four cigarettes, and they were old Chesterfields and Winstons.

Sometime you would get a fresh pack from the SPs just when you had to cross a stream up to your chest. Or it would rain day and night for three or four days.

As a trail got worn through the bush, guys strained to keep their feet under them on the climbs. Digging in was easier, but then you were sitting in a puddle all night. In the trees the most ingenious shelters sprung up from ponchos. Tied at odd angles to trees, roots, branches on fallen logs. I could stay just about as dry just hunkered down under my poncho with the hood on and my helmet on top. Finally, I wake up to fog. The sun burned through and I felt myself warm by degrees. Then I would be dry at last, prewarmed and ready to bake for hours as the day brightened like pulling up a window shade.

A cigarette became like a cocktail after work. Few lit up when we stopped along a trail. Nobody walked along with a cigarette in the corner of their mouth. The Hollywood look. We were climbing most of the time anyway and it was a brutal strain. We smoked after heating up a can of ham and limas or beef and rocks (beef and potatoes) or chicken soup. Seldom did anyone use water from their canteen to make coffee in a six-once juice can. Coffee and a cigarette was a rare luxury. That was living.

After eating a can of whatever, slathered with ketchup or tabasco that somebody in your squad bothered to carry, you lit up and talked about food. Cars and sex were next on the list. The further you got into your tour, the less you talked about the world. Maybe if you had a wife. Otherwise the world became a vague memory. You talked about how much time you had left and what you thought your chances were.

Guys would smoke after digging in. If it was dark,

you had to pull your shirt over your head to make sure the glow didn't give away your position. The blacks craved menthol. It seemed all they would smoke were Salems. One brother got a carton of Kools in the mail. It was like he'd won a numbers game back in the hood. The buzz went all through the company.

My treat is the chocolate disk that comes with the chicken noodle soup meal. It includes a half-size can with crackers and a foiled covered quarter-inch disk of solid chocolate. After I eat and I know we aren't moving out for awhile, I fill a six-ounce juice can with water, get off by myself and take a tiny bite of chocolate and a sip of water. My treat will last at least 20 minutes. You had to have the right C-ration meal, enough time and enough water. Six ounces doesn't seem like much when I think of it now. But I do remember that it was a big luxury and that I took it nice and slow.

The chopper ride seems like a gift from Buddha. God is out of the picture. We sit on the floor as the wind rushes through the open door. I envy the door gunner. We hear that choppers get shot up, but still, that would be the way to go. Cool and easy. We had hacked out an LZ, then saddled up for a ride – eight to a bird – to an adjacent hill. I'm on the first chopper and as it flares six feet above the blowing grass just below the crest of Hill 558, I jump into the crackling of AK-47s. I start firing and moving forward. I'm yelling for the others to get on line. I fire, roll away, load another magazine. The grass is knee high. I don't see anyone on my left or my right. Then it stops. I went by the book. Where the other seven went I don't know. The other birds swooped in, their door gunners blazing away. Dig in. I was sick of digging in. I dig a minimal hole, a post hole I could just stand in up to my waist.

My team leader tells me to get everybody's canteens and fill them at a trickle 40 meters down where the slope levels out. I have them on a belt and walk through the grassy clearing to the stream. As I kneel filling the first canteen, a whoosh thuds into the bank just to my left. It's a dud, enemy, 82 mm mortar round. The barrage erupts up the slope and the 82 mortar rounds and 152 artillery rounds walk along our position. I light up in terror. Do I stay put or run for my hole? The air screams and the hillside explodes. I take off. I squeeze down in my hole, jam my helmet on and my flak jacket on top of it. I open my paperback and press my face into it.

This is by far the most terror I have ever endured. I wait for a screaming freight train to come right down the pipe. Not a trace of me will be found. The noise, the image of a direct hit, the waiting for obliteration, is horrifying. I wait for the impact. Stark, cold terror.

Our artillery from miles away start pounding in on the hills around us. I have no recollection of getting out of my hole, of saddling up. I remember we headed out when the barrage stopped. I walked all night over Hill 881 past friendlies who were sitting alongside the trail every 10 meters or so.

"Hey man, heard Charles shot you off the hill. Where you from in the world?"

All along the line of Marines on watch, "Hey man, where you from in the world."

"Seattle. Where you from?"

"Chi town."

Days later, we come across a section of Highway Nine. Hulks of burned out tanks sit along bends in the road.

We're to provide security for two or three tanks that are making a push for Khe Sanh. We string out along the road and walk. The dirt road is carved into a hillside. Huge boulders jut out along the downhill side. On the hillside across the steep ravine, someone spots movement. Hiding behind boulders and tanks, we peer across the ravine. A band of rock apes, about the size of large chimps, move along single file. One of them stops and hurls a rock down below, then scoots up to the others.

In the mountains, contact with the NVA is sporadic. There are no villages or hamlets where NVA may infiltrate to cache supplies, or use civilians to harbor and supply them. They are a fighting force much like we are – roaming the mountains, hitting and running or trying to dislodge main forces from hills just south of the DMZ. They are supplied by civilians and cadres who work for years, moving supplies down the Ho Chi Minh Trail network that winds through Laos and Cambodia into the Iron Triangle area along the western border of South Viet Nam.

We are supplied by helicopters, Huey slicks or Chinooks. When we make contact, automatic fire erupts and we hit the ground and fire wildly into the brush, trying to locate where the fire is coming from. Squads of Marines fan out and push up through the undergrowth. Occasionally, the NVA are dug in and a pitched battle starts up and we see them running, as a hidden machine gun blazes from behind them. They fight from caves and holes dug into the side of a rise covered by thick forest. Often they are trailer elements harassing us after their company or battalion has moved on.

One morning, I'm walking point ahead of their

squad. Miller and White are next in line behind me. Their attitude seems so different. Not only do I dread the daily humping, and exhaustion, I feel I have little chance of making it home. We walk through a tunnel of thick brush, not sure if we have a flank element out or not until we yell and they answer back.

The hit-and-run type harassment directed at our strung out column leaves me with the feeling that it's only a matter of time until I meet up with a bullet with my name on it. Miller and White just react, just take it in stride – business as usual. I don't know what they know. I don't feel what they feel. This is like a football game to them.

The morning goes along okay. Then a loud whoosh and BOOM knocks me on my face. Then nothing. I get up and take a few steps back. Miller and White are nothing but unsorted chunks of meat laying in a shallow crater. They'd taken a direct hit by our own mortars. Killed by friendly fire. Shock overwhelms me. I stand rooted, staring at their torn up bodies. They should be on their feet, the best soldiers in the bush. They could handle the shit. But not this, not a fuck-up by some officer down the line. What's the retribution going to be? Who's going to pay for this? How could their chances for survival be fucked with like this? How could they be dead? There was no contact. All secure negative contact.

"It's the Nam, man; it's fucked," a flat voice intones. "Better them than you." This scene, this nonchalance, freezes me at the crater they curl in.

Nobody seemed to react. That's the way it is. That's the way it would be. Months later, I would find what was left of a team member in the crater of a rigged 105 round. I thought about booby traps under his corpse. I thought about other mines around him. I thought about the possibilities of landing a medevac chopper. I never thought about *him*. Over.

We keep humping day after day toward Khe Sanh. I started sipping water but not swallowing it. I let it slide out of my mouth back into the canteen. I had no idea when we would get supplied with water or come across a stream. This rationing would cost me later.

I get over fear. When we make contact, I move at it shooting. I prefer walking point. But I couldn't get over the misery of the heat, the terrain and the load I carried. I didn't worry about making it. It didn't matter. I had too much time to go in this killing zone.

I'm cleaning my rifle before moving out one morning. A young-looking kid wearing glasses comes up to me, squats on his haunches.

"The next time we make contact, I'm going to shoot myself in the foot," he said.

"Do you know what a M-16 round will do to all those bones in your foot? You'll be crippled."

"I've thought it out. I'm getting out of here."

He walks away. He was a new guy. For a second though, I thought about where you could shoot yourself without inflicting huge damage. I hold my M-16 behind me with muzzle pointing at the upper part of one cheek of my ass. Seeing if I can reach the trigger.

Once the sham of stopping communism from seeping toward American shores slaps your blinders loose, and the shock of the meaningless waste of lives opens your eyes, a shattered foot, a blown off finger are carefully weighed. Extreme physical hardship and unnecessary death break you down. Thinking, hoping turns inward, focuses on endless agony. Your old world shrinks like a flame on a match head. You want out. Death would be acceptable. Even suicide becomes an option. The future is a forgotten concept.

Mail was important, your only connection with the real world. It would pile up in a rear area, Phu Bai, Dong Ha, while you were on an operation. But one day a red mail bag was dumped out of a chopper along with C-rations and ammo as we dug in along the slopes just under a ridge line. The chopper swooped low over the ridge and dumped a little inspiration. The letter had a picture of my little brother sailing over a makeshift hurdle in the backyard. His form was good. His grin was a killer. I would have to see this. I would have to make it home.

I get a real break on our last hump, the day we finally make it to Khe Sanh. We drop down out of the hills and onto the road that once led from Dong Ha to Khe Sanh and hook up with some tanks for the last push. We are walking on a road. I almost feel cheerful. This is easy walking. I think tanks must be the way to go, but then we go by some that are burned out hulks, the tracks blown off. Holes blasted in the turrets. Some are pushed down the hillside to clear the way. The road climbs and switches back and forth as it climbs.

We're stopped when the hatch pops open on the lead tank.

"Hey man, where you from in the world."

"Seattle. You?

"Oxnard."

"Where?"

"California."

"How much time you got in country."

"Two months."

"Oooh, I got two months to go."

"What's the hold up."

"Waitin' on the word to come on in. We only got two to four klicks, to go. They're going to bring up some more security. Yup, here we go. Want to ride? Just straddle the barrel."

"Oh yeah. Absolutely."

We stop just outside the wire of the Khe Sanh firebase. We're in a wide-open valley. There's a lattice-work of razor wire laid six inches off the ground stretching 50 meters to the coils of barbed wire strung along the ground and then the barbed wire fence. Inside are low bunkers. That's just the perimeter.

I hop down, the first one through the gate. A Marine is standing there frozen and wide-eyed. Then he's nearly jumping for joy. A few more gather at the gate. They seem dingy and pale, but they're overjoyed to see us. I feel like we just liberated a death camp. I wonder how bad it is out here. In the next minute I'm nearly jumping for joy. Insulated cases of hot food are lined up on the ground. A beefy chef is spooning beef and mashed potatoes onto paper plates. I tuck my M-16 under my arm and take two plates heaped with food.

In an instant I feel true pleasure. Suddenly there's another greeting, as the first rounds come screaming in. Guys are still coming through the wire and sprint for trenches. I kneel carefully as I watch one of the new guys sprawl into a greasy puddle of reddish water. The rounds are long, over-shooting our position, and I continue to balance my two plates of hot food.

After a few days, you could set your watch by the

incoming artillery. It seemed to start in late morning for a few minutes and then later in the evening. And, of course, anytime a plane tried to land. There were burned out hulks of C-130 and 131s along the runway.

There were a couple of artillery emplacements and mortar pits scattered around the base. The army had some trucks that had a searchlight and quad 50's mounted on the back – four .50 caliber machine guns. I felt totally safe whenever I stood watch in a bunker next to one of those setups. Notwithstanding the airstrip, most of the base appeared to be underground bunkers connected by five-foot deep, sandbagged trenches zigzagging around the perimeter of the base.

Our platoon had about four of those bunkers. Double bunks had been built of pallet boards in some. I found a smaller, damp one I claimed for my own. It was completely dark and smelled of shit. Someone had left a pile behind. I cleaned it out, stowed my pack against the wall, leaned my rifle near the entrance and laid my poncho on the hard packed floor. It felt like a concrete slab. All I needed were some candles. I didn't have to dig in anymore.

We were picking up garbage along one of the single lane roads that wound around the artillery batteries. Myself and a black guy, I don't remember his name. Picking up some litter I noticed the 155 artillery piece pivoting. BOOM. Shot out. An earsplitting shock knocked me underneath the truck I'd been cleaning up around. I don't know if it's volume, surprise or concussion that sends me flying, but I'm in pain. Scrambling from under the truck to get away, I nearly run over the other guy who is on his knees with his hands clamped over his ears.

The two of us are on garbage detail again soon after.

We steer clear of the batteries. The day is cloudy, but not socked in. We're on a road carrying a garbage can, picking up C-ration cartons and cans. We've already gone over where we're from and how much time we have in. We're poking along. It's just nice to be above ground for a spell.

The spell is broken as a freight train comes screaming out of the air and we bolt for the small bunker with the jeep parked alongside. We beat the round by a split second and the roof comes down on us. I'd landed on top of him. The jeep is burning. He's wide-eyed and dusted gray. Rockets are coming in and there's a huge low bunker 30 meters away. We don't talk about staying put or going, we light out for the big bunker – the command bunker, the target. We can't figure the best time to go. So we just go.

Rounds are raining in and we just hit it. Terror transfers to speed and we're flying side by side as we duck into a low slit that opens into a cavernous concrete underground bunker that turns out to be the command bunker. It's unbelievable. We're on a wide stairway with handrails descending 15 feet below ground. Bare light bulbs glow on this dude standing there holding a cup of coffee and chit-chatting with another guy. The purr of a generator accompanies this remark, "What the fuck are you guys doing here?" I'm dumbstruck by the amenities. What rocket attack?

They aren't at Khe Sanh, they are under Khe Sanh. Babes in a cool womb, biding their tour, waiting to be born innocent. They most likely never got a peek at the Grim Reaper.

One month, Echo and Foxtrot Platoons take turns patrolling outside our wire, getting ambushed then rained on by 82mm mortars. A tank comes out and loads up the dead and wounded. When the B-52s stop bombing, we take up to 600 rounds a day. There are 50 meters between guys on watch in the trench now. Not 10. Well I could have been at Hue City. They take 8 to10 casualties a day for 27 days.

We move to the other side of the base to stand lines. I find another bunker to myself. A better one. Part of the walls are red stone, probably from some wall or building in Khe Sanh Village. I can stick a candle to the stone for reading. I'd seen the village from a chopper once – French built stucco buildings with tile roofs. A stream runs through the village and coffee plantations surround it.

One night, my squad leader comes by for a heart to heart. I think of him as Snuffy. He has this nasal voice and this habit of sniffing that makes him seem dim. He has that good ol' boy, cracker mentality that grates on me. I don't think I was elitist. I worked construction – good, blue-collar, union labor around red necks that I had a lot of respect for. I was a college kid that liked the work and the people. They are hard working and straightforward and good-humored. Snuffy is a cracker, a good ol' southern boy. There is no racism in the bush. Color has no bearing regarding trust or cutting it in the bush. But this is my second dumb cracker for a squad leader.

"You know," he sniffed, "you're always readin' books, and the guys wanna know why you never play cards er nothing. Why don't you quit readin' books all the time and be more like the guys."

"I read books cause I don't want to be like the guys. Besides, I'm hoping it keeps me from becoming stupid."

Sniff. "We'll you otta just try to be more like the guys."

Thirty years later, it dawns on me that he was just trying to get a little more unity among his men, probably something a good squad leader should do. But I just couldn't buy into our mission. I'd learned real quick that this war "against communism" was a total sham. An inhumane, wasteful sham.

Chapter Three
Not a Loner Back Then

I was so desperate at my new school that I offered to buy Roy Springer an ice cream cone if he would be my friend.

"Sure," he said.

I was eleven-years old. We went to his house with his friend Dick Burkett. They lived in a poor neighborhood. We played Parcheesi in an unfinished attic—so different from around the dining room table with relatives, like I was used to.

Roy was kind of a sweet kid, but his older brother was a hood – greasy hair, surly, a little scary. Dick was of the same ilk.

We went fishing on the abandoned dock on Puget Sound at the foot of Sixth Avenue in Tacoma, Washington. It was a couple of blocks from the house I grew up in, at least from age 11 on. A fitting environment for me and my new friends—kind of rough like Burkett was. Three other toughs showed up one time while we were fishing—a small guy who did the talking and two henchmen. They had cigarettes. I'd never been around this kind of element.

The little hood said something in a low voice to Dick. Some money changed hands – a dime. The hood and Dick went to an abandoned boat storage shed on the dock. The friends of the hood stayed behind. Dick and the ringleader came back. Dick had a small trickle of blood coming out of his nose. The little hood paid Dick to let him punch him in the face so he could show his cohorts that he was a tough guy. Dick said it took two punches to draw blood.

School started again and my suburban neighbors came out of the woods or from vacation homes or wherever. I joined the Boy Scouts and made friends in the neighborhood. We played sports. I don't think we ever went to the dock.

Chapter 4
Leaving Khe Sanh

I held the candle flame to a spot on the brick wall of the bunker and stuck it to the hot spot. The bricks had been hauled from Khe Sanh Village when the air base was built. They were about 14 by 8 inches and rough-hewn. Once a spot heated up you could press the shaft of the candle onto it and have a nice wall lamp. The quad 50's were next door. I was reading Hemingway when this desperate guy slipped into my bunker.

"Hey Akins. You're a piece of shit. Let's go out and fight."

He wasn't from Charlie Platoon. I don't know which of the other two that made up our company he was part of. We all knew he was claiming he was a Jehovah's Witness so he could get out of the war. He was the classic insecure 19-year-old male who didn't know if he had enough machismo to call himself a man.

He thought the Marine Corps would make him a man, only he didn't want to be John Wayne after all. And he had that inch-and-a-half, block letter, red and blue USMC tattoo on his shoulder. He hadn't had his chance to lay claim to manhood. Hadn't conquered, hadn't been bloodied by war. Probably hadn't ever been laid. He got a peek of war and wanted out. A fight would be his last chance to prove he was a manly man.

He knocked the paperback out of my hands. "Come on, let's fight."

"Against your religion, remember?"

He slapped the book out of my hands again.

"What's the matter, you afraid to fight?"

"Seems like you're the chickenshit. You can't lie about what a hero you were when you get home? Oh, that's right, you'd be the wrong kind of hero, a sinner."

"Let's go up on the airstrip and fight, chickenshit."

I picked up the book again. I wasn't going to give him the opportunity to remedy his insecurity. A dickhead with a tattoo. A dickhead with a way out. This time he didn't say anything as he made a pass at my book.

"Alright." I said giving in. "Sounds like a good idea." It really did, it most certainly did.

We crawled out of the bunker, out of the trench and walked toward the fight line.

I knew he'd try a sucker punch, he did and I ducked it. I charged him and tackled him onto his back, scrambling to get my knees on his chest and my hands around his throat.

He got his legs going, trying to flip me off him. As we rolled I tried to get my forearm around his neck and squeeze like a vice. He was pretty big and rolled us again nearly getting me in a head lock. He didn't have a good hold on me and I was starting to wriggle free. He stood us up and I popped loose. I'd managed to cut off his wind a little and he was breathing hard. I feinted a punch and snap kicked him in the knee at an angle, just like we'd been taught in boot camp. I charged again and as we went down two guys jerked me up from behind and slammed me down. I rolled and got up and they were standing between me and the Witness.

"That's it. Git the fuck back. You are in a world of shit." They kept edging me back. I could just see around them. The Witness sitting, a third guy standing over him, his hands on his hips. I wanted more, I could have gone as long as it took. I wanted to stomp that fuck. I wanted to break his collar bones like they taught us in boot camp. He wouldn't be able to wipe is own ass.

That morning the Captain and I had a talk.

"What's your problem, Akins?"

"He wanted to fight. He kept after me 'til I gave in."

"Well good riddance to both of you. He's going home on religious grounds and you're going to a Combined Action Company. Ever heard of 'em? They're those small teams that get overrun all the time. You get on a chopper tomorrow to Phu Bai."

The outfit I transferred to was called 1st Combined Action Group. The teams of five Marines and a Navy corpsman worked with up to a platoon of Biet Laps, mercenary type or Popular Force soldiers who were more like a militia force. The area of operation was between Da Nang and Chu Lai with Highway One sort of bisecting the area. The terrain was flatter, but the war was up close and personal, real personal.

Chapter 5
A New Way of War

A chopper picked me up and flew me to Phu Bai, our headquarters. The whump, whump of blades on a Huey are melodic, like the sound of a train rolling down the tracks. The breeze through the open side door is fresh. When you're not going into a hot zone, flying below tree tops, it's a nice ride. You cover territory effortlessly. This is where you see how beautiful Viet Nam is. The dense, deep green mountains that look purple at twilight. The shades of green – rice fields, bamboo, jungle vegetation I'd hacked through, slipped through and hid in but never learned the names of. The South China Sea glitters between blue and green and is fringed by white sand – nothing on it but beached fishing boats.

I had a barracks to myself while I waited to be processed out of Echo Company, 2nd Battalion, 1st Marine Regiment, 1st Marine Division. I slept on a cot, no mattress. It was the first time I hadn't slept on the ground in four and a half months. Plywood shacks dot the landscape. Some have refrigerators and clerks at typewriters. Eight-man dusty barracks await infantry companies that may get back to base to recoup for a few days.

Along with the mess hall, the cots were quite a luxury. Mountains loomed further in the distance and the whole place had a dull red tinge to it. In one shack, a Vietnamese barber gave me my second haircut in-country. I had a mustache, the first one I'd ever grown. It came in thick and curled at the ends.

The place seemed deserted. Choppers came and went from the LZ. The artillery battery fired missions. There was an enlisted men's club, a bigger plywood shack with a bar and a few tables. It had a reel-to-reel tape deck. I went there once and drank one formaldahyde-treated beer. I watched four black soldiers do a sort of line dance to the rock instrumental, "The Horse." It looked cool, dancing side-by-side in sync, moving rhythmically. Flashing big smiles. The Marine Corps provided my introduction to soul.

I got a package from home on June 8th, my birthday. A blue, quart Purex bottle filled with whiskey that was sealed with a melted Styrofoam plug. Sitting on the cot, I contemplated the odds of getting this on my 21st birthday. I mixed some warm Kool-aid with a double shot in a mess kit cup for my first legal drink. No one was around.

I got another beautiful chopper ride to the Marine base at China Beach near Da Nang and the headquarters for 1st Combined Action Group.

With CAG I went through a couple days orientation to get a basic idea of working in liaison with villagers to get their cooperation to slow infiltration by NVA and Viet Cong. They would know where the enemy was and how many. The Vietnamese soldiers we worked with would soften the barrier between us and the civilian population.

We would protect them and win them over to our side. Each team had a corpsman who could tend to civilians on "medcaps" as well as saving wounded and dying Marines. Teams would establish small compounds in an area near hamlets and villes where the Viet Cong and NVA operated. Looking back, this was probably the only effective effort U.S. troops made toward preventing a communist takeover.

During orientation, we fell in each morning for a little briefing about the day and then went to class. Bill Jameson, a corporal, was on his second tour in Nam. He was from Atlantic City, played football at Ohio State and had a wife at home. We hit it off and ended up at our first assignment together at CAP 1-1-1 outside of the town of Tam Ky along Highway One near the coast. Later, we would butt heads. Bruce Barr, another transfer from a battalion in Eye Corps, was a tall machine-gunner from Brooklyn. He'd been transferred to CAG after being treated for jungle rot on his feet. He stood in formation rocking side to side ready to grin at any moment. Barr would end up at CAP 1-1-2, a neighboring position a couple hours away from my CAP.

The week ended and guys were sent to various outposts. Barr and I, and a guy named Dean, were sent to a CAP on temporary duty while we waited to go to our respective assignments in Quang Tin Province. I was back in the bush. We got there in the evening and the squad leader told us we were going on patrol around 4 am.

It's was a hot area. We were replacing three dead Marines and one wounded. We got to the site and a corporal, the squad leader, lined us up and told us we were going on patrol at 0400. A lieutenant from headquarters had come for a visit, checking on his troops, I guess. The corporal was acting all gung-ho, talking in clipped militarese, showing off. It seemed like stateside shit.

"I'll need a radioman." He points at me. "You!"

"You carry the gun." He points at Barr.

Months later Barr and I would hook up again as replacements on a team that had lost half the squad in an ambush.

"I'll take point. You're next with the radio, then you," the squad leader points at Dean and Barr.

Barr is in the middle with the M-60 and the lieutenant is in back with the rest. We leave the compound in darkness and walk through sparse jungle along a trail. Such easy going, I think, flat and open and walking on trails. This is like walking through an arboretum or something. We come to a little clearing and stop a couple steps into the open. It has low, dirt berm walls on three sides. Hmmph, I think. We stop in the open? It's still dark.

The corporal walks up to me, looks past me at Dean.

"Where are the others?" he whispers.

He waves Dean up, asks him. Dean looks back and shrugs. All of us had come from grunt companies up north and are used to moving in long, loosely strung columns punching through solid forest and jungle. You watch behind if you are walking drag, rear security.

"Wait here, I'm going back for the others," and the squad leaders goes off down the trail.

Wait in a clearing? I reach for Dean's shirt as I crouch and whisper, " This is no ...." and bawham, rrrrrrrrooowww... The explosion is a ball of light at my feet. I feel a blow like someone had swung the point of a carpet hammer into my forehead. Muzzle flashes pour from the other side of the clearing. I pull the trigger on my 16. Nothing.

"Dean, I'm hit. My rifle won't shoot," I'm yelling

above the roar of his M-16. It all stops as suddenly as it started. I think I'd been shot. A dam bursts and bathes my face in warmth. I'm still alive, I think. Dean thrusts his rifle in my hands. I grab the hot barrel and drop it. Dean whips off his green T-shirt and is winding it across my forehead. The pain zeros to a fine point in my head and my neck burns. The others run up. Shrapnel jammed the bolt of my 16 and cut the tape antenna off the radio. I'm still on my ass. Barr runs up, starts laughing.

"Hey man, you got hit."

Somebody said, "That's his third heart. He's going home."

It isn't. The lieutenant tells the squad leader to call a medevac. The human head is full of veins. So much thick blood pours out of the scalp of my hairline, the door gunner starts putting a battle dressing on my chest. I don't tell him I didn't get hit in the chest. At the field hospital in Chu Lai, a young doctor stands at the gurney I'm lying on and removes four pieces of shrapnel from my hairline and puts in a blanket of stitches.

"Look," he shows a corpsman the petri dish with the bits of metal as if he had better things to do than trifle with this.

"Chicom. If this had been U.S., they'd be bagging you."

I fall asleep on the gurney. A little later, the corpsman wakes me.

"We need the gurney."

I'm naked. My boots are on the floor. I look around for my pants and shirt, find them in the garbage can and get dressed. I'm wearing a gauze turban and soggy clothes.

"A truck's coming to pick you up. Give 'em this."

The corpsman hands me a slip of paper. "You have five days light duty in the rear."

The truck comes. Five days out of the bush. I'm starting to feel okay. Five guaranteed wake-ups. I nod to the driver and hand the paper to a tall, craggy-looking first sergeant with big glasses. He drives me to the Chu Lai LZ.

"Your going to CAP 1-1-1."

"Whoa, I have five days light duty."

"They give you some Darvon?"

"Yeah," I said, taking the bottle out of my pocket.

"You don't need no five days skating in the rear," snorts the lifer.

I would meet him about eight months later and refuse to be his body guard.

The squad leader at my new team is a dick head. He has a catalog of leisure suits, the polyester one-piece things blue-collar retired guys wear. He orders a color for each day to wear when he gets home. He has me go on two-man killer team my second night with a Vietnamese militia type.

"I'm supposed to have five days light duty in the rear."

"Those doctors are always trying to let people skate. You're going back in the bush."

Jameson was there. Barr had gone to 1-1-2, a few klicks away.

The squad leader shows me a map marking our area of observation, then brings out his gallon jar of fingers and ears.

My first experience being around a sadist.

On ambush a couple nights later, I'm so spooked I'm in agony. Shadows creep up on me. Bushes rustle. I spend a night in pure panic.

There was this dumber-than-a-box-of-rocks idiot at this pos who bought one of those black, flat-crown cocksucker-cowboy hats in Chu Lai.

"We should all get these and have them embroidered with, 'just you and me, right God?," he beams like the moron he is.

"I might get something that asinine, but I fuckin'' doubt it, dippy."

He narced me to the squad leader, one morning after I'd worn a pair of Levis out on a night ambush.

"You can't wear those. They aren't military issue."

"They're comfortable lifer boy. You got a problem with that?"

I ran into Cowboy Hat later when I refused to be the first sergeant's body guard and they sent me back out to 1-1-1 or 1-1-3 while I was waiting to rotate. My rotation date was delayed while I was under investigation for murder.

I'll get to that story later.

Anyway, this asshole with the cowboy hat had been in Chu Lai in supply. My footlocker, which was stored in the supply tent, had been broken into. Some NVA items, some Korean jungle utilities given to my by a ROK soldier and my Purple Heart, were gone. The dippy cowboy at 1-1-1 was wearing the utilities. They weren't that easy to come by. I knew where he got them.

Then he fucked up guiding in, by radio, a resupply chopper that was in plain sight in the middle of the day. He had them pissed so bad, they said fuck this and flew away. I missed a hot meal.

The asshole was wearing my stuff, and on top of it, he fucks up a resupply with hot food on board. I'd had it. I tried to get him to go out with me that night on a two-man killer team. I told him I'd take point and have my back to him. He wouldn't go.

You don't buddy-fuck another Marine. It's against the code. You don't fuck up a hot meal for someone who can count the number they've had in a year on one hand. That could have been a medevac chopper. This could have been a hot LZ. I'd been in the bush thirteen months. I'd seen too much, done too much. What's another kill? Nothing to me.

At CAP 1-1-1, I meet Harold Mason, a 19-year-old blond kid from Delaware with a sunny disposition. He is a true ambassador to the Vietnamese.

"Let's go have tea with the villagers," Harold suggests.

We sit in a thatched-roof hut made of bamboo walls. A cooking fire is in the center of a hard-packed dirt floor. A low wood bed covered with a straw mat is against one wall. A low-slung hammock cuts across another corner. The lukewarm tea has green leaves in it. The only tea I'd ever drank was some Lipton with a piece of toast when I had flu as a kid.

"Drinking something warm helps keep you cool," Harold advises. He's smart for a 19-year-old.

Kids hide behind each other and peek in the doorway. Someone shoves one inside and a high-pitched cacophony of chirping erupts. A kid with two inches of hair that sprouted every which way grins.

"Marine number 10," spiky head quips a put down.

More chirping from the others. Vietnamese rate everything on a scale of one to ten, one being the best.

"Marine number one. Beau coup number one,"

another replies with authority.

"Marine number fuck!" Spiky chides.

The hive of brown-skinned imps buzz around the doorway as Harold chats with mama-san. It's like he is visiting with an auntie or something.

This is my first time around civilians. I'd been in country almost five months and never encountered the people. It didn't occur to me to compare their lifestyle to what I grew up with. I didn't feel that they were lacking. By their demeanor, they aren't. They appreciate our gifts of cigarettes or C-rations, which they mix with rice and offer us. Their lives are simple – hard work to reap what nature offers, and raising children. And they revere their children. At this ville, they harvest fruit, raise pigs and chickens. They gather bamboo and sell it in the town of Tam Ky.

It didn't occur to me what it must feel like to have foreigners with weapons dropping by the neighborhood. I guess they are used to it. At a CAP I am assigned to later, when a patrol comes to a village, we are given chairs to sit on in the center of the village for viewing by the villagers. Except for the village chief, none of them has ever seen Americans.

At the small compound that comprised CAP 1-1-1, most of the guys built a bunker for themselves.

One guy – I can't remember his name – a wiry, pale guy, stayed in his bunker for hours. If he wasn't on a patrol or ambush, he stayed in his bunker. He was a diligent soldier. They said he stayed in there and smoked dope. Another team member, Ralph Avila, was a dark, Hispanic with a wife and two daughters. That amazed me, that someone so young would be married, much less have kids, and be in the military, and in a war on top of it.

Joey Lisa was a gregarious, blond-headed nineteen-year-old who needed his front teeth straightened. He was from West Virginia. Years after being home, I got a call from him. It was 1978, and my girlfriend and I just walked in the door after a night dancing at a tavern. The phone rang and it was Joey Lisa. He was married with two kids and worked in a coal mine. He was the only guy from the war that I'd talked to – just that one time – until 1999 when I went to the Veterans Administration for treatment. I hadn't given any of these guys a thought. I had erased, or tried to erase, that whole experience.

It was so odd to hear from Joey – that he would think of me enough to chance a phone call. Had he been going through some Viet Nam memorabilia and found my name and folks' phone number on a scrap of paper? I told my girlfriend how odd it was to hear from him, out of the blue. I'd kept in touch with my main partner Barr for a little while, but only thought about Viet Nam at night, while lying awake. Or when the shadows around a construction job on night shift drew me like a moth to flame. I'd walk from the corner of a five-acre fenced yard of a construction site to the parking lot at lunch break and never leave the shadows under the modules' floors that were seven feet off the ground. The temporary lighting on poles cast deep shadows on the of the two- and three-story metal buildings. I pictured Joey in a cool, dark underground shaft. There's something comfortable about darkness.

Yeah, for Joey to call me felt odd. I'd distanced myself from the whole thing. Viet Nam was something I did, and then moved on. It is still something I pretty much avoid. When Joey called, Viet Nam was my secret. We only talked a couple minutes. How's life? Fine. How's it going for you? Not bad. We didn't talk about the others. We didn't talk about the weirdness of being back from the surreal, no-taboo world we shared for a couple months. If Joey had been part of a family that could afford braces, he could've been the blue-eyed handsome man in a uniform. If Harold had been a little taller, he would've been a Marine poster boy. Both probably wouldn't gotten embassy duty in Panama or Europe. Handsome features, perfect teeth.

When I first got to CAP 1-1-1, Jameson was all business. Going for more rank. Harold and Joey were cool and it felt good to be tight with somebody. If we weren't on ambush or patrol, we'd share radio watch at night. We wouldn't talk much about home, mostly how fucked up the war is and the close calls we'd survived. How brutal the mountains are in the dry season and how cold they are in the wet season.

The enemy contact we made seems small time after the Khe Sanh hill fights. Incoming would be a 61mm mortar round. If they ambushed us, they were gone in seconds. Around here we deal with Viet Cong. They are not as well equipped as the NVA.

It's here that some officer comes out and pins a Purple Heart on my shirt for being wounded earlier.

"Well, I'm glad somebody is mixing it up with them," he said shaking my hand.

Mixing it up out there? Oh yeah, I forgot, combat is like a football game. You're scared until that first hit? Where did these clueless officers come from?

Jaco, our sadist squad leader, was hauling his catalog around trying to encourage us to order those one-piece leisure suits. That's two guys at 1-1-1 who are into nerd fashion.

"You should get some," he says.

"Why, so I can look like a geek?"

One night, I leave the wire about midnight. Just me and two South Vietnamese soldiers. I figure they might know a good ambush site. I radio in the coordinates. I'd been up most of the previous night on a team ambush and I can't sleep much during the day. My legs ache. My eyes ache. I start to hallucinate. I spring back as a huge orange giant came around from behind a bush. I shake my head trying to get clear and focused. Then I see a gook skimming along the surface of the stream on a motorbike. I call the compound.

"One-six this is nighthawk, over."

"One-six, go."

"Be advised I'm coming in. I'll be at the wire in 30 minutes, over."

"Nighthawk this is one-six, over."

"Nighthawk, go."

"Be advised you are to stay in position til daylight, out."

"One-six, this is Nighthawk. I cannot stay out here. I'm seeing things, unreal things. It's not safe. I'm coming in."

I collect the other two and head back. I'm not trusting my senses and I'm not taking any chances.

"One-six, this is nighthawk, over."

"One-six, go."

"We're coming in. We'll be at the wire in 10 minutes, out."

"Nighthawk this is one-six. Wait one."

Jaco got on the net. "You do not come in.You stay the fuck out there. Out."

A few minutes later we are crouched outside the gate and I radio we are coming in. I get to the command bunker in the compound. Jaco comes striding over. "I told you not to come in."

"Well, I was hallucinating," I said as I shrugged the radio pack straps down over my arms.

I don't see the punch. He catches me flush on the side of my face, and I'm seeing stars and flashing specs of light. The radio is half way down my arms as I wriggle out of the shoulder straps. My M-16 leans against the side of the bunker.

I don't know what I would have done if he hadn't rang my bell. With an M-16 handy I had the advantage. I could've butt stroked him easily. It was minutes before I came out of the fog. Jaco had whoever was on radio watch the rest of the night keep an eye on me. Later that morning Jaco left on in-country R&R, a last minute arrangement. I'm not sure what I would have done, had I gotten the opportunity.

I was transferred before Jaco got back from R&R. I wasn't yet at the end of my rope like when I came across that cowboy hat fuck who broke into my footlocker. But it's dangerous to punch another Marine in the bush.

Still, maybe I was lucky. I've heard that psychological difficulties are worse for those who lose their restraint or their morality during combat. I had lost much of mine. How much worse would I have been if I had fought or killed Jaco, or killed Cowboy Hat over a pair of pants. Over a medal?

Chapter Six
Monkey on My Shoulder

Four of us were milling around the deuce-and-a-half parked alongside CAG Headquarters in Chu Lai. Ralph Avila, Harold, myself and another guy from our CAP team were waiting for a ride to the LZ in Chu Lai to get choppered out to 1-1-4, a new CAP position near Tam Ky.

Headquarters was just a few Quonset huts, a few plywood barracks, the small mess hall and the mail shack. The mail shack was where a first lieutenant was "killed in action" by a black dude who didn't appreciate the lieutenant's quip about looking for his court martial papers. A full magazine, one split-second burst point blank and the lieutenant was gone, KIA. The truck driver gave us this news.

I'd met the lieutenant. He was older; I wondered why he hadn't make captain yet. But he didn't have an attitude, just a decent guy. I'd talked with him once and liked him. The lieutenant was a white-haired, red-faced avuncular kind of guy who was filling in for the mail clerk while he was away on in country R&R. I'd heard about in-country R&R, but I'd never come across anyone who'd been on one. I heard you went to Da Nang and got your brains fucked out. I think the Rear Echelon Motherfuckers [REMs] were the ones who usually got plenty of R&R, inside Viet Nam and outside.

I seldom got to the rear, so I went to the mail shack, a 10-foot by 12-foot room with a counter and maybe a wall of pigeon holes. There was a flap board to get behind the counter. I pictured the scene of the lieutenant's murder. Did the killer reply, "fuck you honky," and blow him away? Or did the rip of 18 rounds of .223 caliber say it all? By this time I knew I didn't want to be in the rear, even though you got hot food and sex with slim, saucy Vietnamese girls, or quiet, patient but stern ones who could cut off the romance in a minute and push you lovingly out the door. They were all beautiful and young. They really should have brought some out to the bush. At least once a month. Yeah, we would have had something real to die for then.

The four of us discussed the murder and were just waiting. A jeep pulled up and the driver got out with a small monkey perched on his shoulder. The thing was a cutie with big eyes beneath a high forehead. His thin lips were pursed in that "oh so busy" like expression. Except when he'd grin and pooch his lips out at us. The guy came over to us and we all went through the how's-it-goin'-dude, where-you-from stuff, while the critter bounced from one shoulder to the other, peeking around his head, scoping us out.

He sat hunkered down on his haunches, back curved, body hunched over. His head swiveled from side to side watching all around. He seemed busy just sitting there. The monkey pulled the guy's hat off and dropped it for the dude to catch. I stood next to them while his pet pawed his head with his tiny, preternaturally human-like hands. They had wrinkles, creases and fingernails just like ours. Its hands were about the size of small toddler's. Maybe a little longer and skinnier. And they could fly. He'd spread a patch of hair down to the scalp, waving his hands over the spot, then dig through another spot, his fingers skittering over the short parts formed by the hair being spread apart. His little fingers flew. He'd pause, then scramble over to another spot.

"Want a massage?"

"Sure, man."

He nudged the monkey off his shoulder onto mine. It couldn't have weighed much more than 3 pounds, and it felt good sitting there. It scooted from my left to right shoulder and back to my left. Then I felt it's little fingers rummaging through my hair lickety split. The pads of its little fingers felt great on my scalp, maybe a cross between tickling and massage, but really fast. Flying fingers, then a pause, then the fingers working furiously. It felt good having my hair parted and tugged a little as it searched for bugs. Since I was in the bush all the time, my hair would get pretty long. I couldn't hear any chomping or crunching, but I figured if one little hand left my head, he was having a snack. Or maybe he threw it away.

"Feels pretty good, huh?"

"Oh yeah! Where'd you get it?"

"Traded a case of C's for him up in Dog Patch, up in Da Nang."

A driver came along and we got in the back of the truck. Just as it was leaving, a pogue (office worker) came out of the office and yelled, "Akins get off the truck. You've got orders for language school in Da Nang, dude."

"All right Johnnie boy." Harold clapped me on the shoulder.

"Thirty days in the rear with the gear."

"Take it easy out there Harold," I said. "I'll be back."

The next time I saw Harold, he just had his lower

right leg amputated in the field hospital in Chu Lai. He'd asked for me and I got choppered in from the team I got sent to after language school.

Ralph Avila had been with Harold and me and Joey Lisa at CAP team 1-1-1. Avila was this dark-haired, handsome guy from California or Texas, I can't remember which. The guy with a wife and two young daughters. He was killed in the attack on 1-1-4. While Harold was on watch in the trench, Avila was in the bunker with the four other Marines that were killed. Joey Lisa stayed behind at CAP 1-1-1. He made it home, probably rotated from 1-1-1.

Lisa was a good natured blond-headed Okie, except he was from West Virginia. The three of us – me, Harold and Joey – stood last watch together around 5 a.m. and listened to Armed Forces Radio. We listened to rock tunes and worked on our dance moves. The sun is just up, a big orange ball teetering on the edge of the world. The warmth feels good. When you're not under attack, the mornings are so fresh and clean. Not crisp. Gentle. Soft and beautiful.

The jungle, the bush, is most beautiful on a dry-season morning or clear night on watch in the compound, a full-moon night that was so bright I easily read a book. Even the shadows are beautiful—sharp, deep purple contrasts melding into breaks in the jungle.

Chapter 7
I Get a Break

Today I can look up the names of all the killed and wounded on a CAP web site on the date it happened.

It happened. Just like the officer in Khe Sanh said it would. A CAP where friends of mine operated got overrun.

"Akins. Get off the truck. You've got orders for Language School in Da Nang."

This is how I was spared. I'm on the truck, then I'm off the truck.

I didn't even know about language school, much less put in for it. But instead of getting overrun at 1-1-4, I spend thirty days on a Marine Base in Da Nang studying Vietnamese. The thought of a month in the rear makes me feel giddy as I grabbed my pack and weapon and jumped off the truck. "Hey man, *han gap lai,*" Harold says good luck in Vietnamese.

The school was at the Marine Base at China Beach. The schooling was adapted from the Defense Department language program, so a 10-week crash course is crammed into four weeks. We have Sundays off from noon on. We take a quiz every day. If we flunk one, we are sent back to the bush.

We sleep in small barracks on thin mattresses on metal framed bunks. I'd been trying to learn a little Vietnamese from any of the Biet Laps we worked with who spoke some English. I scored high in language proficiency in boot camp testing and almost got sent to the three-month language program at the Defense Department facility in Monterey, California. But it's early 1968, and they need riflemen up by the DMZ. So, no chance at Monterey for me.

China Beach has a mess hall and teenage prostitutes outside the wire. Guys sneak under the wire at one corner of the base. A hooch (hut) with a mama san and a young girl are about 15 meters from the wire. Five bucks. I don't have it. We don't get paid in the bush. The money stays on the books. I never got any. I pleaded with the mama san, begged her to no avail. I'd been in the bush. Downtown Da Nang is a few klicks outside the wire. I never make it.

I work hard in school. I want to get something out of this whole experience and learning the language is the only thing that seems remotely possible.

Chapter 8
Some Send Off

A chopper comes out and picks me up from 1-1-7. Nobody says what's going on. A trip to the rear. Okay. At the LZ in Chu Lai a guy is waiting in a jeep.

"Harold asked to see you. He got fucked up. They got overran two nights ago. Part of his leg got blown off."

What do you say to a boy who's going home from a war maimed? Harold is 19. When we were both at 1-1-1, we used to go to the hamlet together to visit with the villagers, drink tea with them. This was his idea, just go in for a friendly visit. Once he borrowed a bicycle from one of the Biet Laps (Viet Nam militia) and rode to Tam Ky to get a block of ice for the water jug. He'd gotten some packets of Kool-aid in the mail from home. We liked to stand watch together, just to shoot the shit. Blond-headed, smiling Harold was a sweet, sweet kid.

Whenever a guy gets wasted or fucked up, the survival wisdom is, "better him than me." I repeat that to myself as I walk into the "hospital," which is just a long plywood shack crammed with narrow beds. It's like a long corridor with beds along one wall. Harold is propped up. I see bloody bandages just below his knee.

"Hey, how are you doing?"

"Okay I guess. Avila's dead."

Harold looks resigned, not all that happy about going home. That's the thing. If you got shot up and a joint was messed up, but not blasted or shredded, going home was great. It's something else when part of you is left behind. You're going home, but part of you is lost. In 1968, there is nothing heroic about missing limbs. Unless you plan on staying under the shadow of the military. Living in the fantasy of sacrifice for your country. Harold's wonderful, innocent, sweetness seemed dimmed – a 100-watt bulb reduced to 20 watts. He had this incredible innocence about him. He didn't get jaded. He took stuff in stride. He was not an intense guy. I didn't feel bad in the hospital. I couldn't. Could not. You don't feel if you want to survive. I thought about Avila's wife and two daughters. I felt honored that Harold wanted to see me before he left for the states. I don't even know how Harold made out. I don't even know if he's still alive.

I couldn't think about Harold and me in a ville drinking tea with the mamma-san. I couldn't think about Harold strapping on a prosthetic.

Harold talked about how he got wounded – how his leg had a huge hole in it. I told him it was good he still had his knee. But he wasn't even out of country. By the time he made it to the states, it might be gone to the hip.

"Avila and Harvey are dead."

We'd been on the truck to go to a new CAP position that wasn't even completely built yet. It wasn't ready. I didn't think about whether I'd be dead or maimed. What's it like to be overrun? Seven Marines and a squad of South Vietnamese against about 40 NVA. I knew it was more like seven against 40 when the shit hit.

I knew Harold wouldn't get medals and the hero treatment. He was a nobody. Just a Marine grunt, a Private First Class. An unknown. He could fight with a cool hand. You could count on him in the bush. He was just a nice, easygoing kid. He never hated. He was a lover. He had a light heart. Officers didn't know PFCs. They didn't hang with PFCs. Lance Corporals and Corporals carried the radio and drove vehicles for officers who were in the field.

CAPs didn't have officers in the field. The CAP officers commanded from headquarters, and headquarters was in the rear with the gear. Harold went into the Marines at 18 and went home maimed. He would have to deal with it on his own. If Harold stayed sweet, if he stayed straight and sober and could rise above the anti-war venom, then maybe he's still around. I hope so. He's one of the gems I met over there.

Guys get killed. Nothing new. But Ralph Avila had a wife and two daughters at home. How could he be dead? How could a father with two kids be sent to Viet Nam, when others could skate just by going to college? What will his wife do? Why do they send a father with two kids to the bush?

What does it mean when a teenager asks to see you before he goes home a cripple? Harold is laying there being Harold. He's not being stoic, but he's not crying, not pissed off. He's calm, but I can tell he's scared.

He tells me matter-of-factly what happened. They were hit, hordes streaming across the open ground through the one strand of wire around the perimeter. Harold's alone in the trench and someone jumped in the trench with him.

"I hesitated, I couldn't tell if he was Popular Force (PF,friendly Vietnamese militia) or Viet Cong."

"Then I saw he had a grenade and I rushed him, grabbed him. I tried to turn him. It blew and killed him. I looked down and my leg had a huge hole in it. I pulled the dead gook on top of me and hid until the gunships showed up."

Four Marines are dead and one is wounded.

"What were the PF's doing?"

"I think they pretty much *di di-ed.*" (Took off.)

I couldn't help staring at the place where his leg should be. A soldier's worst nightmare. Some soldiers had pacts with each other. "I'm going whole or I'm going home dead. Make sure of it."

He looked so sad.

A few months later, a chopper is sent out to pick me up again. I have no reason for going to the rear. Again I'm in that long, low plywood shack with the narrow corridor crammed with beds full of maimed guys. It's Jameson. We meet again. We'd been at CAP 1-1-1, my first team, together. We have some common ground. College. He'd played freshman football for Ohio State. Later, he came out to my last team. He came to take charge and those of us who established the team and started the compound were used to having no one in charge. We ended up like two silverbacks in the same patch of jungle. I did some behind-the-scenes maneuvering and Jameson got transferred. But that's a story for later.

He's propped up in the narrow bed. Land mine. One leg is gone above the knee, the other is tore up pretty bad. Later it would be amputated.

"I talked to my wife this morning. She said, 'I don't care if what's left of you would fit in a matchbox, I want you home.'"

"You're a lucky man, Jameson. You have a hell of a wife."

He's trying to make himself feel whole. He's trying to put spin on a picture he's well aware of. There will be little respect offered him. He has a loving wife to go home to. But I could tell he was scared. He wouldn't be alone, but he would be. He would be a guy who went to war, a war his peers find ways to avoid.

I believed it was better to be over there unattached. But I realized why it was good that Jameson was married. He was a dedicated soldier. She would be proud of him. She would love him, no matter what.

Still, he would be alone. His sacrifice was huge, but it would be diminished. The majority of the American public would offer him a cold shoulder.

Chapter 9
Lovely Killer

I was getting something. I was learning the language. When I got through language school, I was sent to CAP 1-1-7 with two other Marines, Barr – who I'd met before at CAP training, and another guy. We were replacements. Three Marines had been hit by a remote-detonated land mine and then shot up. KIA.

1-1-7 was remote, only accessible by chopper. It was east of Tam Ky, not far from the Truong Giang River. It was located on a slight rise in an area that looked like jungle spread over sand dunes. It was the first time I'd seen cactus and coconut trees together. The area changed between jungle-like flora to scruffy pine forest. But '7 had an interpreter, a Viet Namese soldier who spoke and understood English. I shadowed him everywhere practicing, practicing and listening to him bitch about conditions.

"I going to leave here. This no good. I have to sleep on ground. With army I have cot and mattress."

He wasn't around long. He got himself transferred back to easier duty with the U.S. Army.

Barr and I got reacquainted and got tight. He had a couple of joints.

"If we're going to talk about getting high," he said, "we need a code or something. Like, 'do you want to do something nice?' Or 'is that guy nice?' "

The third guy who came with us was nice. This was the first time I'd smoked since the summer I spent in the University District before reporting to boot camp. The three of us went outside the wire supposedly to take a shit. We squatted in a line and got nice.

Seven was a much hotter area than 1-1-1 had been. That is, we had no trouble making contact with the enemy.

We left the compound one morning with the bluest sky washing over white sand. The jungle wasn't so dense. We were still in Quang Tin Province, but closer to the South China Sea. Short, dark evergreen-looking trees, Banyan trees and stalks of cactus turned the terrain into more open jungle.

The patrol meandered along, not following any paths. We took a break. The squad seemed a strange lot. Three crouched together in a circle lighting up cigarettes, talking. Why aren't they spreading out? Why isn't someone watching up front. Why isn't any one covering the rear? I separated a little and sat leaning against a tree, watching the gentle rise of sand before me.

The stillness went BAWHOOM. A spray of sand flew up to my right. A black blur streaked across my line of vision and I fired a burst. Someone to my left fired too—the corpsman. Everyone was flat on the ground. I thought someone to my left had sat on a mine, but no one was hurt. It was dead quiet. It was too big a blast for a Chicom grenade.

We moved up the rise. The others went back down to watch the area up ahead, leaving Barr and me standing over a young barefoot girl, about 16 years old. She was wearing nothing but a black shirt and loose black silky pants. She had a cartridge belt around her waist with one American grenade on it. An American M-2 carbine lay on the sand a step or two behind her. I see this image today like it was yesterday. Powerful. She was the first female combatant I'd seen. Her shoulder-length hair was tied back. A few wisps of hair stirred alongside her face. She lay on her back, her eyes closed. Beautiful, with delicate features. Perfect skin. One layer of silky clothing. Some thirty years later, I would connect with this scene.

I never cared that she wanted to kill us. I still see her lying on the sand resting. I'd been in country seven months. I couldn't comprehend a beautiful young woman who was out to kill.

Thirty-two years later, I wonder what had her family been through? Did the Viet Cong kidnap her? Did a political officer fill her head with duty, loyalty, patriotism, turn her into a killer? She looked like a sleeping beauty. Alone and very brave. The sun was very bright and the sky a deep blue. The sand she lay on was white and soft, hard to run on.

We carried her to a good ambush site and pinned a cruel note to her silk shirt. We hid in the tree line and opened up on the sobbing soldiers who found her.

Chapter 10
Six Can be a Beautiful Place

I was lying in my hammock when they assaulted us in broad daylight.

At 1-1-7, I discovered how comfortable a nylon hammock is.Both ends is tied with a single rope, but with no spreader bar to keep it wide open. When I lay in it, the sides came up and snuggled me tight. I slept in it for six months whenever I spent the night or part of it in a CAP compound.

The Biet Laps had built an open-sided shelter with a tiled roof in the center of the compound. The small compound was ringed with bunkers that were connected by a trench. Barbed wire and some concertina wire surrounded the perimeter. The shelter looked like a picnic shelter at a park back in the world, but it was dug down a couple of feet and lined with sandbags. The Biet Laps would laze on grass mats or in hammocks, sometimes two to a hammock. I had my hammock in there, reading one day when the assault started.

Automatic fire pours in. Most of it directed at the squad leader's bunker, which is clearly marked by the whip antenna on the radio, and at the .50 cal machine gun perched on top of a bunker down the trench line. I spill out and run hunched over to the 50. I'm assigned to it, it's my baby. I call it Susie after the song "Susie Q" by the rock group Creedence Clearwater Revival. Belts of ammo are linked up and nestle in a can attached to the side of gun. A .50 cal is a huge machine gun with a five-foot barrel. The base plate and tripod weigh 100 pounds. The rounds including the jacket were about seven inches long and as big around as your index finger. The butterfly trigger is at the back of the gun between two vertical suitcase grips. It's fired with two hands and the barrel swivels.

Crouching behind the bunker, I have to reach up to open the breech and lay the end of a belt in and close the breech. I hesitate. I'm afraid I'll get my arm shot off if I reach up to load a belt. Then I do it, I get right up on the bunker with it. I open up and sweep the barrel back and forth in a wide arc. I beat out a rock rythm to Gimme Some Lovin'" by The Spencer Davis Group. I swing the barrel side to side and watch the small trees in front of the compound get mowed down, and then it's over.

The squad leader runs over. His eyes are as big as quarters.

"Akins. I thought you were a shitbird, but you saved us."

Barr and I start to saddle up to check out the tree line. They'd opened up from the tree line directly in front of us, about 70 meters from our compound.

"We're not going out," the squad leader says.

"What do ya mean," Barr said. "We gotta check out that tree line."

We end up going out by ourselves. What we find is scary, a real eye opener. They had dug a trench right at the edge of the tree line, right in front of our compound. We stare in wonder at the sand bags they'd lined it with.

We haven't been at seven very long, but it becomes clear how things are run here.

"These guys have not been patrolling man. They've been staying in the compound," Barr said.

Fuck, I think. Been here a week and get assaulted in

broad daylight. If they'd taken out the 50, we probably would have been overrun.

"We're in some serious shit here, Barr," I say.

One-One-Seven was not too far from the Truong Giang River and Ky Phu Village, a small fishing hamlet along the South China Sea on the other side of the river. The first time we went to the village, they brought chairs out for us to sit on in the center of the village. A big crowd gathered to see Americans for the first time. I remember one guy seemed like a freak. He had to be 6 foot, seven inches and solid. The kids finally got bold, laughing and pushing each other toward us. They pulled on the hair on our arms—weird hairy humans.

In the Fall of 2000 I went back to Ky Phu village. The village was bigger and spread out. There was a cabana set up on the beach serving beer and soda. They'd rigged a couple of freshwater shower stalls in back. There was a roped off area where you could park your motorbike. Paid parking. It was a small Vietnamese resort. A crowd gathered. The kids whose parents could afford to send them to school could speak English.

Before the war, every kid went to school, now only those who could afford it. I tried to speak Vietnamese after a 32-year lapse. Even back then, my Vietnamese was limited. So I was probably talking gibberish and they laughed.

They pushed and shoved each other toward me and giggled. The bold ones would pull at the hair on my arms, the same as before. I loved being there. I felt happy. The blue ocean curled in onto the sand that was still pure white. To the north there were woven-reed, 16-foot fishing boats on the beach. Huge nets were folded inside.

The beach, the boats – it looked the same as 32 years ago. I went up the beach toward the area where CAP 1-1-6 had been, where I'd spent the last five months of my tour. 1-1-6 had been formed by three of us who never returned one day from a 1-1-7 patrol. We found a spot we thought would be a good site for a compound and some of us stayed.

I walked up the beach. I found what I figured was roughly the area were Keig got killed by a rigged 105 mm land mine and Cronin got his foot blown off by a toe-popper. I looked up the beach and recognized the curve of the beach that was five or six klicks north of 1-1-6's position.

I followed a footpath into the interior. It was bright and hot and felt good. The ocean, beach and jungle came together like an image of paradise. It was so pristine. I felt spooked. I went a little bit further in, but I was afraid of mines. There are still a lot of unexploded mines and dud artillery rounds left from the war.

I stood in the quiet and tried to understand what I felt. I was happy that I was back in this exquisite setting, that I was not here as a killer. Still, inside my chest I felt a flicker of excitement. I felt a buzz of fear in my balls. Waves of attraction and repulsion washed over me. The spookiness of war was there, but it felt serene. I could take in the beauty without the tinge of danger. It was hot and deserted and it reminded me of the isolation I felt ever since coming home from the war.

I was standing in the place I worked hard to put behind me, but could remember like it was yesterday. I was in the surreal world where I'd come face to face with evil. I felt good, relieved.

But I was frightened. Scared that demons would rush me, pull me into their dark world. I was standing in the jungle where life had been so tenuous and so devoid of meaning. It was just about killing and surviving.

I think there will always be an unreal air about it, the beauty and the horror of it. I felt some relief, that I could be there and not be associated with the evil of war, of killing, killing, killing. I walked back to the beach and shuddered in the strangeness of being back here. I was looking back into my secret, and I was feeling both frightened and peaceful.

A year later, I returned and went further north along the beach, to the rise where the 1-1-6 compound had been. I looked at the curve of the beach far ahead. Some day, I want to spend the night there. I want to go further north to the Phu Yen fishing village where I fought so often with the North Vietnamese Army and the Viet Cong. I want to hear children laugh at my Vietnamese. I want to honor the dead there. I want to look for my soul there.

Chapter 11
We start 1-1-6

There was a little pop. It was the starting gun and the prize was our lives. The guy to my right stepped on it. I heard it and took off sprinting and launched myself onto the sand. The explosion was huge. Out of the corner of my eye, I'd seen the guy on my right take off too. He was lying on the ground big-eyed and shaking. Unhurt. If the detonator had been rigged to go off instantaneously, we'd both be dead.

It was the first time we'd gone on patrol across the river. We went into Ky Phu ville and linked up with a platoon of Biet Laps, South Vietnamese forces. Barr, Arnold, myself and two others went on the patrol. Our squad leader and a couple others stayed back at 1-1-7. It was a big sweep up the interior between the river and the ocean on a narrow spit of land. We headed north from Ky Phu ville. The kids here were much healthier than the ones I'd seen around 1-1-1. Doc said the sea provided a better diet.

It was a daytime operation with about 20 Biet Laps. We spread out and swept north, trudging through the soft sand. We plodded through a deserted ville and jungle that turned into cactus and a scrubby pine forest. There were a couple more big explosions with columns of black smoke rising out of the ground. The Biet Laps that set them off had not outrun them.

Sometime later in my tour, in this same area, I would get lucky again while looking for a lost Red Cross worker who left a celebration at Ky Phu Ville. I'll tell that story later.

Two more black columns of smoke rose from the ground as we continued our sweep. About five klicks north, we found ourselves on a small tabletop rise. It had good sight lines ahead of us. I could see up the river on our left and up the beach on our right.

I turned to Barr. "This would make a good place for a position."

"So why don't we make one, stay here right now."

The three other Marines in the patrol were getting ready to head back to 1-1-7.

"Me, Barr and Arnold are going to stay. We're forming a new position."

The Marine got wild-eyed and shaken. "You're crazy. We gotta get out of here."

"See ya."

I borrowed a radio from one of the Biet Laps and radioed headquarters with our coordinates and told them we were staying to start of a new CAP. We would need sand bags, ammo and C-rations and a PRC-25 field radio. There were CAPs 1-1-1, 1-1-2, 1-1-3, 1-1-4 and 1-1-7. We didn't know about a five or a six.

"Be advised, our call sign is One One Six," out.

I called the army artillery battery we used and told them of our new position and gave them our coordinates and call sign.

"We may need you tonight, out."

Our headquarters, at least the mid-level guys, didn't like this idea. I didn't realize until later how much I agitated them. A private first class making decisions and plans like that. It would get worse. The Vietnamese District Chief liked it, though, so we got the supplies we wanted. I woke up about the third morning and a large Vietnamese work party was there to dig the bunkers and lay razor wire up and down the slope and a barbed-wire fence around the compound. They worked all day and accepted Salem cigarettes and C-rations with gratitude. I practiced my Vietnamese and did a little digging too. I gave an old man with missing teeth a Salem. He grinned then looked at it for a bit and started picking little tufts out of the filter thinking this was how to light an American cigarette.

We got it going before anyone was there to take charge. Resupply choppers didn't like to land here. Downdrafts could set off mines. We'd go back to 1-1-7 if supplies got too low. We had our own place, way out where no one had been before. We had no fucked up supervision. No supervision whatsoever. Arnold was an E-4, a corporal. I was E-2, private first class, and eventually made E-3, lance corporal, but not for long. As the mid-level guys got more agitated with our freedom, they would find a way to get me busted back to E-2.

Our first patrol was up north to the long curve in the beach that we could see from the top of our bunker. We didn't go up the interior; mines made it too risky. We found an opening into the jungle and several bunkers, mounds of sand about four feet off the ground. The place seemed deserted. Our radioman asked if he could borrow my .38 revolver.

"I want to check out some bunkers down there," he said pointing deeper into the jungle. I handed it to him, then knelt and studied the map.

A minute later, I heard, "Help. I can't get back I'm pinned down."

It was the radioman. Some NVA slipped up near

him, probably intending to capture him. They didn't fire him up on the spot. I couldn't see where he was so I jumped on top of a bunker to look. A figure slid into view. I fired a burst and saw him fly off his feet. The others opened up and our radioman came sprinting up the gradual slope and kept going. We followed him to the beach and kept sprinting. I looked back and saw a group firing at us. I caught up to the radioman and grabbed the hand set.

"Stop. I gotta' call in a fire mission."

He kept right on going. The spiral cable from the handset pulled tight and the connector popped out of of the radio. The cable came whipping back at me.

After our first contact with the enemy, our corpsman panicked. When we got back to the compound he said it was too dangerous, we were outnumbered and the AO (area of operations) was too remote. He got himself out of there and said he had the authority to get us out. He didn't. We wouldn't. The new corpsman from the old outfit joined us. He adapted real quick—a good crazy corpsman from Montana named Brasille or something.

From then on we made contact every time we went up there. Many of our contacts were during daylight and up close and personal.

Something was changing in me. It was subtle and I didn't notice it at first. I wanted to go up there often, and I liked that the stakes were high.We would get shot off the beach again. But the spot became like a magnet. It was like the urge that consumes you after the first time you went all the way with your girlfriend. You wanted more. Nothing else mattered.

Chapter 12
The Thing About War

We tried just about every kind of guerrilla tactic we could think of. Whatever we had seen in the movies, whatever we imagined. It was our ball game and we coached ourselves.

Fishing boats appeared in the area where we always made contact to the north. The soldiers we fought up there were mostly NVA. They were in full uniform and well equipped. This was in a free-fire zone, so we sniped at them with the 50 cal and once called in artillery. We noticed when we sniped at them or called in a fire mission, the boats made it back to shore at breakneck speed. I couldn't believe how fast they got back to shore just paddling.

The Navy patrolled our coast line with fifty-foot Swift Boats. I got into the habit of swimming out to them even when the sea was rough. They had chocolate milk, steak and strawberries. I'd swim out to them and see barracuda flash through the light green waves. These craft had a 81 mm mortar and a 50 cal machine gun, firepower that we relied on.

One day, they sent a skiff in and took us up to the area where the fishing boats would appear. I swam under the surface and found hemp ropes four to five feet under the surface stretched from shore outward. This is how 20-to-30-foot double-ended fishing boats could get back to shore so fast. They'd snag up the rope and haul ass back to shore. I didn't try to find how the ropes were anchored out in the bay. The Swift Boat was idling in enemy territory close to the beach, with me in the water.

Were the NVA fishing? What was going on up there? I led another patrol up there, got into the same collection of bunkers just inside the tree line, and again the fight was on. Smitty was new to the team. We were spread out, returning fire. Smitty was next to me, flat on the ground. I was on my knees building a bomb, a satchel-like charge out of C-4 wrapped around three grenades, tied together by det cord. I crimped a short timing fuse into a blasting cap with my teeth and jammed it into the ball of C-4.

"I can see them," cried Smitty.

The automatic fire was cracking in and Smitty and I were still in the spot where we'd hit the deck. We didn't have much cover.

"Just keep shooting," I yelled.

I almost had it all together.

I waved everybody out and told Ooten to cover me where the trail exited onto the beach. I moved up behind a bunker, crouched there with my Zippo ready. When the others fell back, the NVA started moving up. I lit the fuse, peeked around the edge of the bunker and slung the package up in a big arc, grabbed my rifle and lit out. There was a huge explosion.

Ooten was on a tiny dune alongside the trail at the edge of the beach covering me, but with my camera! I'm hauling ass expecting him to lay down cover fire and he's shooting pictures. We were running down the beach full tilt when the NVA made it down to the beach shooting at us.

Down in Ky Phu village the fishermen had small, circular woven-reed basket boats about four feet in diameter. I got the idea that we should try to insert into this ville at night from the ocean. Paddle in quietly from an unexpected approach.

We tried them out, using a single paddle to see if we could maneuver them through the surf. I lost my M-16 when I tipped one. Lost it in six feet of clear water. The pogues in the rear try to charge me $136 for it. No dice.

One night we launched the little boats, four of them, and paddled north. Once we got past the line of breakers we made pretty good headway. All we took were M-16s, no radio. We wouldn't have any backup, but we definitely would have the element of surprise.

We got to our insertion point and paddled into the breakers. From there we got out of the boats, which we couldn't control in the surf and swam them into shore. We moved quietly into the tree line, spread out and waited. We were submerged in darkness on a cloudy night. The tree line was a band of blackness in front of us. I knew they had no idea we were in their backyard.

I watched with my M-16 on my hip. A flash of black broke in front of me and I fired two shots. A few minutes later, I heard moaning. The waves washed rhythmically at our backs. We peered into the site of two previous firefights. Moaning rose and fell about 40 feet in front of me. I slipped over to Barr.

"Maybe we should go on in."

"Let's wait for a little daylight."

The darkness turned a bit gray and I moved in and saw a form on the sand with two dark shapes hovering over. I'd hit a sentry. A woman dressed in black silk pajamas lay with her leg split apart from knee to hip. Two huge, low-bellied pigs had their snouts in her wound. Her flesh was all tore up. She began moaning again. Without a radio I couldn't call in a medevac. Even if I had, this was a hot area and we didn't have much fire power; we probably couldn't secure the area. Precious time slipped away. I'd fired two shots. We couldn't stay. It was almost light, we would have no cover. We couldn't take her with us. Shooting up the pigs would announce our presence if the shots I fired hadn't already. We couldn't sit in an area where we were heavily outnumbered. The pigs were feeding on her leg. You can't freeze time and think it over. I couldn't think of an option. This was supposed to be a hit-and-run. We were on our own in an area controlled by NVA and Viet Cong. We had to hat up. But leaving her felt hellish. I went back to the team.

There are so many things that I have kept buried, that I would go to my grave with. When I came home there were so many reasons why I wish I hadn't come home.

"We don't have any choice here. Pigs are feeding on her. I don't think she'll live. Can anybody do this?"

No takers. I went back to her. Then we quickly left.

Chapter 13
Le Thi Tuyet

When I first went back to Viet Nam, I found a "girl-friend" there.

Tuyet wakes up in my arms, this 85 pound little bit, in a seedy little hotel in the middle of a coven of two story apartment buildings wound all through the back alleys of Pham Ngu Lau district in Saigon.

"Uong kafe?" she asks when we wake up in the morning.

"Drink coffee?"

She slips on my shorts which barely stayed up over her narrow hips and droop at her 16" waist. She puts on my T-shirt and tosses me my pants to dig out some money.

"I like your outfit," I'd say. "You know the baggy look is very hip in the states."

"Uua," she utters the Vietnamese phrase for agreement.

She comes back with two plates of food, sometimes on a silver platter, stuff she buys from sidewalk vendors. It is so tasty – barbecued duck, soup with chunks of beef and little hard-boiled bird eggs and shrimp, rice and tall glasses of black coffee on ice.

"You go to restaurant, very expensive, no good," she scolds. I sit on the edge of one bed and she perches on her heels on the other bed, using my suitcase for a table. It intrigues me the way she crouches comfortably with her butt on her heels, her feet flat.

Every exterior wall of every building in this maze of

a neighborhood is a shared wall. It's dense back there. The alleys are the width of a sidewalk, yet motorbikes weave around the crowd of people sitting in doorways and walking wherever they go. You have to look carefully to find an entry way off the street into the interior of this maze of back alleys. The rooms in the hotel are often shared by hookers. A room might have three beds, a shower and a small end table and that's it.

A family lives on the bottom floor. If you go in late at night, family members are asleep on the tile floor, and one or two on a low futon bed. The family altar will have fresh incense. There may be a computer. There will be a modern TV. There's a small kitchen at the back. The stairs are narrow and you have to duck your head where a corner of a landing extends into the stairway.

Tuyet has a raspy voice. She smokes cigarettes. You don't see young Vietnamese women smoking cigarettes unless they're hookers, and the chances are they smoke heroin. They believe nicotine enhances the high. She has three feet of long hair. That seems rare for young women in Saigon today. Many of them have short western cuts, many with red or blond streaks.

She doesn't wear a hat or long sleeved gloves, or wear a bandana over her face like most women do to keep the sun off her skin when she's on a motor bike. She doesn't worry about her skin getting darker. She's from the Mekong Delta not far from the Mekong River in the city of Can Tho. She pronounces Me Khong, "May comb."

"Some day I take you to May Comb" (Me Kong Delta), she promises.

I've hooked up with her two or three times when I've gone back to Viet Nam. The last two times, I took her with me when I traveled around. Other vets I know, expats who live in Saigon, warn me about girls like her. Their Vietnamese, English-speaking girlfriends are scandalized by my relationship with her. Why would I hook up with a tramp when there are so many decent girls who speak perfect English and who want to meet a foreigner, they wonder. They all know some. I've met them.

Mothers who own cafes introduce me to their daughters. Businessmen that I get to know want to introduce me to their sisters. Viet Kieu are Viet Nam nationals living in the U.S. Some of them I know in Seattle want me to meet their aunts or sister-in-laws. But the ones people try to set me up with wouldn't want to go to a disco. They wouldn't want to swim in the ocean.

Tuyet jumps up and down like a little girl, beaming and hugging me when I asked her to go dancing. Likewise, when I jokingly suggested going to the beach, going swimming in Nha Trang, a resort town north of Saigon, I was sure she wouldn't. The day we went I didn't know she'd gone out and bought a swim suit. I didn't understand what she meant when we got there and she said she was going to go change.

I caught her on camera coming back, running toward me in a pair of jeans over a swimsuit, her long hair swaying side to side. She shucked them and went right into the surf with me, even though it scared her. She had a tight grip on my arm and turned her head and covered her eyes when waves broke at our knees.

She doesn't have much. She's a street girl with a raspy voice and a bad habit. But she's got so much passion. She's not in a hurry when it comes to sex. She orgasms frequently.

"I like you take long time," she coos.

I don't have to restrain her the moment I come. She'll spread her hair across the pillow, lay her head on my chest, fold up into my arms and go to sleep. At the beach lying together on a beach chair she sleeps in my arms while I read. She, curled in my arms asleep, is something I cherish.

I know I could have this with a better class of woman. I also know something would be missing. The dark night. This is part of my legacy from Viet Nam. I was twenty years old when my meat was on the line day after day. The formative years. I was caught in the underworld of combat, when the future was just another wake up.

Maybe it takes a junkie to connect with one. My fix had been adrenalin. My drug spiked with the possibility of death. I acquired an instinct for it, for fucking with it. There's a seductive lure to taunting death. Back then, once you're crawling side by side with evil, the high stakes make the danger more attractive. Tuyet takes me back to a mind-set where I flaunted death. In a way she may be doing the same.

She doesn't worry about what people think. She has an attitude. She grew up knowing life is a battle. She started selling bottles of water on the ferry in Can Tho at eight years old. She didn't get to go to school. She can't read or write. She learned what she could do to survive and not to expect too much. She's tough. She's independent, she trusts herself and probably no one else. And she is sexy. I know she will break my heart.

Tuyet has no idea that she is another connection to the war for me, a conduit back to the dark night. She can't comprehend that I want to save her. I realize that I associate her with the attractive, young Viet Cong woman I killed when she threw a grenade at our team as we paused outside an abandoned ville near CAP 1-1-7. Thirty years later, I'm making love to her corpse, or the part of me that is dead is.

Way back then, it started as a routine patrol.

It's about 9 a.m. It's already hot. I sit down with my back against a tree. Another guy, maybe Fred Callefi, sits a ways to my right. The others are spread out. I remember thinking that no one is paying attention, keeping watch. I'm watching an expanse of sand and scrub brush on a rise in front of us. Suddenly, an explosion rips the quiet. I think Fred has tripped a mine. There's a flash of movement in front of me – a figure sprinting and I fire.

I remember seeing a black blur go down. I'm talking about the young woman with the rifle and grenade again.

I'm stunned by how young and beautiful she is. The idea of a woman soldier shocks me. It's hard to believe that a girl can embrace this kind of danger, that she can bring herself to kill, that she can act on this kind of desire. I can't imagine it. She is so young and exquisite looking. I feel a strong sexual attraction surge through me and for a moment I wish we are alone. This shocks me.

Today, I understand the connection between taboo and sex, that combat and death became sexual for me in the war. Back then I didn't realize I was getting close to the threshold to "that dark night." I didn't know that was how it worked, but I knew I'd changed. I felt different. I knew something had happened, but I didn't understand how.

I know that Tuyet knows that her lifestyle is dangerous, is destructive. Flouting safety, courting death still feels seductive. Being with her had a double impact.

With her, I walk the edge again and flirt with danger in Viet Nam again. It feels good. On top of it I want to rescue her. She's a foxy, wounded bird. I want to save her. I'd killed a lovely young Vietnamese woman, and now I loved one who was living dangerously.

Chapter 14
I Cross Over

The opening in the jungle, with those first few bunkers and the hooches deeper within, became an irresistible fascination. I'd fallen in love with the Vietnamese Goddess of War. She crooks her finger, and I came like a dog ready to go fetch. The firefights were orgiastic but the climax was escaping death again. This would be the most alive I would ever feel.

I was tight with Barr. I believed I could borrow luck from him when mine was low, and he could do the same with me. I believed this. I was a firm believer in luck.

The morning was quiet and lazy. We were staying in, taking a day off. I wasn't thinking about our next patrol or ambush. I wasn't thinking about getting out of here. I'd walked down to the beach with Barr. The surf rolled in on the deserted white sand, rumbling and whooshing back and forth. Our piece of the world was so remote. We were detached, even from the military. If we got resupplied with food, water and ammo, it came from far away by chopper. If we called in artillery, it came from miles away. We never saw those people. We never went to the rear. Headquarters people never came out here.

This morning, I was in my head. Something became real apparent to me. I realized my love for the dark goddess was taking me deeper into unknown territory. I wasn't just living in a different world, a world without taboo. I was a different person. It was hot out. Hot and lazy. Our world was bright blue and quiet in the jungle. The other Marines were down at the well just outside our compound. We were doing nothing this day. We were in a hot Area of Operations and ran the war the way we thought it should go, and it worked very well for us.

When they tried to send a sergeant out to take charge, I couldn't handle it. I had the only master I wanted to follow. Only she could lead me. It was hot and very quiet out. A bright day in the jungle with the deserted beach. I couldn't get something out of my head. I liked it here. I didn't want to be in the rear with the gear.

I'd rather be in the bush like we were, out here in a hot area with no one in charge, than have an easy skate in the rear area.

I'd rather take my chances out here. I felt strange. I couldn't make sense of it. I knew the war was wrong, that it was a complete waste, but I knew that nothing mattered anymore. I never thought about tomorrow or going home. I was addicted.

Years and years later I understood that life is at its highest level when someone is trying to take it, when they can get it in an instant. You may see it coming and you may not, but the instant it could be over is always there in combat. That's why the firefights, the up-close fighting, is so exciting. When you live like this, tomorrow is a long way off. Your world shrinks.

There's no room for the future. You look at it day by day. Your other world and its dreams are gone. You live for the flood of adrenalin. You are at the highest level that you can live. If you cross the threshold into this world, you're changed. You don't think rationally, you need risk. You love walking the edge between life and death.

Chapter 15
A Connection

"Are you the guy that wore the red shorts made from a nylon mail bag?"

The message came to me sometime in the winter of 2000 on the CAP Marine Web site, where I'd posted my name. Someone thought he'd recognized my name and the shorts would definitely confirm his memory.

I hadn't worn them but a couple of times. I had them sewn in Ky Phu ville out of a red nylon United States Federal Postal Service mailbag mainly to flout a federal law—desecrating federal property. Well, they were light and looked good. I also had a cut-off jean jacket in my wardrobe. It went well with the pair of Levis I'd scrounged from a Red Cross donation I'd come across.

Stan had come to six from 1-1-7 to be the assistant squad leader along with Bill Jameson from New Jersey, who would be our squad leader. I'd met Jameson during the week of CAP training and I served briefly at CAP 1-1-7 with Stan.

I was floored to learn that Stan lived in the same city as me. I e-mailed him back and left my phone number. I'd done that with a couple other names I'd recognized from the web site but only received an e-mail, never a phone call.

"Are you living near Seattle?"

"Yes."

"I thought I recognized the prefix. I live over by the community college," Stan said.

We got together at his place. He had a nice house in a nice neighborhood. He hung out in his garage and spent his days putting together book cases or working on home improvement projects. The garage was like a bunker. There was a suitcase there that he hadn't opened for thirty years. It was full of slides of 1-1-7 and 1-1-6. There were pictures of me. He's been in sales and metallurgical consulting in California, but walked away from it a few years ago. Couldn't deal with it anymore. He had a table, a couple chairs, TV and a mobile phone in the garage. The table was piled with mail, catalogs and stuff. I recognized right away that this was his bunker. On a nice day he would open the garage door for a short time.

"I remember you guys stayed over in your bunker and smoked dope out of a .50 cal. ammo can," Stan recalled. "And I remember you had those red shorts made."

"I don't remember you being at six," I admitted.

"I came with Jameson to be the assistant actual, and I didn't get high. We stayed in the command bunker and you guys kept in yours."

We traded names back and forth and filled in the gaps for incidents we both recalled. The stories backed up the slides. It surprised me that I had memory gaps about my time at six. Stan showed me pictures and slides that showed unmistakable views from 1-1-7 and 1-1-6 as well as some of the Biet Laps, the South Vietnamese soldiers, who I recognized immediately, especially the one that could speak some English.

He had a slide of me at a celebration down in Ky Phu village, the one where the Red Cross guy wandered off. This celebration had brass from our headquarters as well as the Vietnamese general. There had been an all-woman honor guard armed with shot guns and a large formation of Vietnamese troops. All I remember is the banquet. I sat across from a headquarters staff sergeant and next to the Vietnamese general, who was very pleased that I could speak some Vietnamese. The staff sergeant was livid. Six had been operating outside the influence of headquarters and the mid-level pogues resented that.

"The celebration was for an awards ceremony," he said. "I got a Silver Star for stuff I'd done before I got to CAG, and Jameson got a Silver Star for stuff that had gone on at six," Stan remembered.

"Jameson wasn't at six but a very short time. He may have been on one or two patrols when we made contact north of six," I said.

Sitting in the garage looking at pictures of 1-1-6 tapped into things I'd put away a long time ago.

"You know Stan, I remember hearing I'd been put up for the Silver Star, Bronze Star and the Vietnamese Cross of Gallantry, but it never went anywhere."

"Yeah, there were guys in headquarters back in Chu Lai that killed that process."

"You know, medals didn't mean shit at the time, but now it would be nice to have the Vietnamese Cross of Gallantry. That came from their side. I wouldn't mind having that one."

"See that suitcase over there." He pointed to an old dusty suitcase.

"Anything I have from the service is in there and I never opened it till I dug out these slides recently."

"Do you remember Jameson at six.? Do you remember when he got transferred?" I asked.

As soon as Jameson came to six he tried to get us to operate in a way we were unaccustomed to. Basically, someone telling us what to do. We knew what to do and how to do it and had been at the the top of the activity board for kills, captures and captured weapons for a couple of months. We had this really good team going.

I tell Stan, "I got Jameson transferred. I'll tell you the story. It has to do with a Swift Boat."

"I remember the call sign for one of the skippers," says Stan. "Vanilla Guerrilla," and the skipper was a guy named Coleman from the camping gear family.

"I remember that guy," I said. "I couldn't believe he was in the service and in Viet Nam."

"What are you doing here?" I asked him. "I know you could have got out of this."

He said, "Ah, I just thought I would do my part, see what it was all about."

Vanilla Guerrilla seemed so unassuming, not how I expected the scion of a major corporation to be. He and his crew were efficient but laid back. They would have fit perfectly with six.

"I'd spent the night with that crew before," I tell Stan.

"Fell asleep curled on the steel diamond plate to the peaceful growl of the diesel engines. I'd go into Chu Lai to their base, eat at the mess hall, watch a Philippine band cover rock 'n' roll songs perfectly. I'd sleep on a mattress and wouldn't leave during a spate of incoming. I could tell they were long. I remember the lights coming on and all the commotion. When the swabbies come back in, they see me lying with a sheet up over my head and think I'm a corpse.

One day Allen and I swim out to the boat and spend the whole day patrolling off the coast of the area north of our position. It gets dark on the way back. I called six."

"Be advised we're going to the swifties' base for the night, over," I say.

Jameson gets on the net.

"You are not going in with them. Get back here."

"It's dark, man, too dark to swim in."

"Where'd this guy come from?" asks the skipper.

"They sent him out to take charge."

"I can get you within six or seven hundred meters, but I gotta keep us outside the breaks," the skipper says.

I don't know why I didn't blow him off. I ask Allen if he wants to wear a life preserver or not.

"It will make it harder to swim cause you'll be so buoyant; it'll be harder to cut through the wave action."

He wears one. I don't. The skipper backs in, directing the bow into the oncoming swells. The phosphorous lights up the water when we plunge in, and I feel a little charge of excitement being offshore in the warm water at night. The warmth of the water and the air, the darkness, the aloneness except for the rhythmic chugging of the diesel feels good and the idiocy of it adds a little spice. I can see the dark silhouettes of the sailors at the back of the boat watching this crazy scene. We are wearing shirts, pants and boots.

I roll my shirt into a belt and knot it around my waist. I can feel the drag of my water-balooned, side pants pockets. I swim smoothly through the swells, lifting my head on the swells to check on the size of the dark band of shoreline. Allen waddles over my way and we head for the rising and falling black band of tree line in the distance. I have no point of reference in the dark. I finally get in through the waves and the washing machine surf. The phosphorous swirls around me in the warm moving water.

"It didn't feel scary; there is no more "scary" for me. Fear has long ceased being part of the picture. I'm having a nice night swim in the warm South China Sea.

I told Stan my high school swim coach didn't think much of me as a swimmer. He put me in the intermediate group for the swimming segment of gym. What was this I thought? I'd grown up two empty lots from the local pool, taken numerous lessons under this guy's program. I did all the strokes, except the butterfly, which only swim team members like my brother and sister did.

"How come I'm not in the advanced group?" I asked the coach.

"You're not very strong in the water," he said.

I don't know how many trips I made to swift boats and back during the four months I was with 1-1-6, but I felt pretty strong in the water then.

That night the swells shifts into the breakers and I try catching waves to get a little push to the shore. I wonder how Allen is doing. It's impossible to keep track of him. The rollers turn into a churning mash of white water as they back up against the sudden rise of shoreline.

I put my head down and dig away. As I struggle out of thigh-deep water onto the beach, I crouch and scan the breakers for a black dot. I thought it might be easier to spot him in the white mishmash of water, but I knew he would have a hard time in a life jacket. There's no sign of him. I wade back in and start fighting my way back out to the breakers. I stop and look around every few strokes, lose ground and then dig for the breakers.

I get through the washing machine water and scan around on the peaks of the rollers. Diving under the curl of the breaking waves spikes the excitement flickering in my chest and gut. It's warm, dark and rough under the crashing water. I pop up, scan and dive. I know he is past the swells, somewhere between the breaks and the washing machine. Finally I spot him bobbing like a cork making little headway.

"Do you want to ditch the life jacket?" I say.

"No," he gasps.

"I'm gonna grab your jacket and swim with you. Just go hard when we get between the breakers."

We thrash our way through the breaking water and the section of mishmash. Allen looks a little shook up. I wonder why the tree line doesn't look all that familiar. I can't see the break in the tree line that led to the rise where our compound is located.

I don't know whether to go north or south. We definitely want to be south of our position. Anything north, you want all your guys and all your weapons. It's all NVA and Viet Cong. I duck back down to the water's edge and scan the tree line. I can't recognize our location.

"Okay," I said. "I'm going to go North for about 300 meters and come back. Don't go anywhere."

Allen had loosened the ties of the life-jacket, but was still wearing it.

"Keep that on," I said. "You look like a black shrub, man. Stay in the tree line. If you see one guy coming your way, it's me."

I recognize the area where we got ambushed when were first established six, and I know we are north. I head back and find Allen waiting.

"Okay. Let's move south.. I'll be about five or six meters behind you. Stay close to the tree line."

And we find the opening in the tree line to six.

A few days later, I come across the district chief in our compound. I tell him our new squad leader isn't a good fit for our team. We can't operate as well. The Vietnamese chain of command takes care of it and a chopper comes one day to take Jameson to his new assignment."

That's when he warned me. He sticks his finger in my face.

"Akins, you'll be working for me someday."

Chapter 16
What Violence Does to You

Spend enough time in combat, feel death and maiming hover around still nights and bright days like crows around trash, and you slip into another world. This is where mores, instinct, luck, or taboo scramble meaning and skew your will to live. Land mines blow men into pieces. There are days of humping 60-pound packs in suffocating heat, long days and short nights, digging in and standing watch until death seems a welcome respite. How?

Exhaustion, the utter waste of lives and the inability to make sense of the military strategy in guerrilla war where the enemy drifts in and out of a fight like vapor. You may end up on a journey to what became known as the dark night, or wrong side of being human. Fatigue and dejection compound the weirdness of coping in a world never before experienced by American youth. Civilians are killed, their homes burned because a sniper hides in their village, picks off one or two Marines and disappears.

Troops die without getting hit—die inside. Their inner selves get killed in action. Zeroed out bodies go home in bags, while survivors, with their emotional being no longer intact, take their new understanding, their new meaninglessness home to a haunting exile.

Combat is where your mind is stretched like taffy sinking into loops. Surviving day-to-day sharpens meaning to a fine point on a steel rod held to a grinding wheel. Too fine and the point can be easily damaged. Too fine and the point is gone. The meaning of life is reduced to a minimum level of existence – just make it through the day; wake up in the morning. Start over. Because the troops in Viet Nam were not old enough, not seasoned enough, not wise enough to know what survival would cost, they stuck it out. The consequences of refusing to go on are not trivial – court-martial, brig time, dishonorable discharge.

Some who haven't experienced a quagmire like Viet Nam think those who did had a choice. Throw down your weapon, take the next chopper to the rear, wait for a court-martial, go home. Young soldiers are not that rational.

We obey, band together and try to survive. We're sucked into a quagmire already roiling in mind-bending shock—a bizarre, inconceivable reality. Meaningless death and maiming. On top of it, this dark world snarls young minds, snuffs faith, drives hope beyond reach. Taboos are broken, have to be broken, are meant to be broken. John Laurence, a former combat TV newsman, writes "that insanity becomes an asset."

Insanity allows them to keep trying to swim the muck. Some boys bail before they get near the edge. Fear overpowers sense of duty, erases images of John Wayne-like fantasy. An infantryman shoots himself in the hand with a .45. Another suddenly discovers he's homosexual. A Marine Jehovah's Witness "sees the light," urgently needs to heed his faith's doctrine against war. His church gets busy and he gets a ticket home. Saved. You met this guy earlier. We had the fight on the Khe Sanh airstrip. He had a big USMC tattoo. I bet he has more war stories than any squad of guys who were there for the duration. But smart. He had an out and took advantage of it.

For those with youthful honor, former dreams fade as a bizarre substitute begins pulling them; a cliff edge beckons. We get over fear. We go numb inside. We forget hopes, goals, the American dream. The danger doesn't matter, we start to groove on the excitement. Living on the edge becomes addictive. We see too much, do too much. After awhile one lingers at the edge of the abyss, thrilling a little. This is where you meet evil face to face.

A fucking new guy who is stricken with fear and cowers when a quiet day or still night explodes into chaotic terror becomes accustomed to the dying and maiming all around him—boys torn apart by land mines, zapped by snipers. He gets past the site of dead civilians—women, children, old men, young mothers. Livestock. With time some check out, become unresponsive zombies while others become ferocious, aberrant, and eager for battle. At best we are not psychotic, merely deranged – just right for combat.

Each contact with the enemy rivets us to the chasm's edge. Thrilling us. If we're afraid, we're gone. The gruesome whorl pulls us in. Purity lost. Civility smoked. We heroically retrieve a wounded or dead friend, assault a position like a crazed maniac. Seeking out any chance to get some juice is the new meaning of life. That boot–camp harangue we smirked at comes around. When the shit hits, assault their ass.

The change is incremental, comes from distance from our first world and in direct proportion to the insanity we're exposed to – friendly fire, murder, watching fear turn a man into a zombie. Mines that evaporate half of a man, booby traps that shear a limb off, days and days of casualties. Eight to ten Marine casualties a day for twenty-seven days during the battle for Hue City. Just don't damage the Citadel.

Guys get jaded. Demented 20-year-olds collect

fingers, wear ears on a string. Around a bend in a trail, a skull on a stake greets the point man. Rocket attacks turn a bunker into a smoking tomb. Gore flies as a round goes through a teammate's skull. Friendly mortar rounds shred three teammates into unrecognizable pulp. Better take it in stride. Deal with it. Numb out and drive on. Can't even tell I'm slipping.

Is this good management training or what? Get to the top. Dig in. Real-world problems and decisions seem pointless and trivial. Young leaders who last a year in combat never want to lead again. Officers who serve six months in the bush go back to the rear. Rear echelon duty – away from madness – that's where you punch your ticket for the corporate world.

Grunts in the bush have to face two brands of danger – the enemy and your buddies. Can the guy next to you handle the shit? Will he freeze up, or will he stay on line, move when you move up and pour it on? Can you trust him more than a short timer who is close to his rotation date, a ticket on the big bird back to the land of the giant PX? How long's he been in country? Is he good in the bush or a fuck up? Is he a stumble bum who will give away your position, get you killed? If you're hit, would he leave you out there seeping out slow?

What's trust about back in your old world? With the people you work with, invest with, fall in love with? It's nearly meaningless compared to combat. People fool around with it. In the bush, trust means survival.

Chapter 17
Trust

The South Vietnamese troops, for the most part, just wouldn't fight. They survived by avoiding trouble, and we were looking for trouble. They would initiate an ambush too soon to scare off the enemy. They could hang back and let us take the risks. I resented their attitude, but I understood it. It was a way to survive. If we had prisoners, that was a different story. The Biet Laps become bold; they shoot tied up prisoners point blank.

After awhile we just didn't take them with us on a patrol or ambush. We left them back at our compound where they stole our cameras, ammo, whatever.

Incompetent or arrogant American leaders from officers down to squad leaders who caused unnecessary death or injury became marked men like buddy fuckers. Some had a bounty on their heads. Fragging [using a fragmentation grenade to kill or wound one of your own] or the threat of it was a way some officers were gotten rid of. It's impossible to tell where a grenade comes from. And troops became students of the grenade as a booby trap.

Ordering a couple Marines to swim through the ocean at night from a Navy Swift boat is not a reasonable order. There's no sense to it; no need for it. This is a problem to be dealt with. A man like this could get you killed.

A squad leader who punches a Marine who comes in from a night ambush early because he's hallucinating is not someone you want to work with. Killing and death become matter-of-fact and everybody is armed.

You were lucky if you had a squad leader who had a lot of time in the bush. He knew his stuff, he followed the code and he would work around a fucked-up order. If a lieutenant or captain wants a four-man listening post outside the perimeter in a hot area, and the squad has been up for two or three days straight, a good squad leader will protect his men. He will have his men set up a short way from a base camp or the main body, call in the coordinates the officer wanted and have half his men bed down.

Good squad leaders learn how to circumvent poor leadership. Good officers realize that the enlisted men who have been in the bush a long time know what they're doing. They run their orders past the salty ones and let experience advise them. Handling people up the chain of command becomes another survival skill that doesn't transfer well in the real world. Back in the world, you may get a job done sooner and cheaper but if you step on toes you're caught in the pettiness of office politics and you just can't cut it.

The bond that makes men tight in combat can never be duplicated in the real world. The intimate closeness of trying to keep each other alive can't be achieved in other scenarios. Not even in marriage. This adds to the void that becomes part of your altered psyche when you come home. Add the resentment of being duped by your government and you're not likely to be a good apple-polishing, trusting employee. Unless you find a job that lets you work on your own and a boss who lets you do it your way, the work world becomes a source of friction.

In combat trust is pure. This level of trust is rare in the real world. But you long for it and it's upsetting when you don't find it.

Chapter 18
Mucking Along

I spend a day – one down – hope for a wake up, an easy wake up. That's it. Life is simplified. Enough water, not too much rain, not so hot, enough food, enough ammo, some less brutal terrain. Days may be unmercifully hot, climbing and hacking through impenetrable mountains. Night can be brief and ghoulish in triple canopy jungle.

There were days when it was a strain to take one more step, days when the death and maiming of guys around me was so oppressive I started to waver, started to accept death as a viable alternative. I've talked to vets who were humping the hills in I-Corps, up around the DMZ who talk about feeling like that. Like it was the Bataan Death March. Another day may be slack, a walk in the park, nestling in thick grass next to a clear running stream. A C-rat chocolate disk with sips of water. Taking tiny, slow bites. Savoring it.

An unfiltered Pall Mall survives stream crossings in a plastic case. We stop. Who knows why, who cares? This is a bonus. I lean against the root of some gigantic, ageless tree with my pack under the crook of my knees; legs weightless. I'm sitting in a recliner in a pristine patch of peril. Not a bit of strain. Muscles slack and senses off track. We haven't had contact in a while. I don't care if they can smell it, it's late morning and I can smoke this without a shirt over my head to hide the glow. I will shut down my sharply tuned senses and try to recall pleasure, bask in it. Maybe this is how a massage in Bangkok would be. I drag on the Pall Mall, slow and deep, playing with the jet of smoke escaping my lips—up, down, around a half circle. Focused on an easy smoke, a full firm Pall Mall. Filtered sun rays warm the grease from 87 days of C-rats spilled on my camouflaged thighs. My pants are practically waterproof. I haven't had my boots off since we left Con Thien.

I own one shirt, one pair of pants. After being wounded twenty days later, I will have to dig through the trash can to find them when I wake up naked in an air-conditioned field hospital in Chu Lai. A chilled bloody shirt and seasoned pants, some pain killer and half-hour of sleep on a clean-sheeted gurney before they need it for a fellow grunt. Maybe the best sleep of a thirteen-month tour. My only in-country R&R.

So many years later, my mind brings back memories of chirpy mornings soaked in sweat, rain-burst afternoons followed by glorious sunsets. Exotic, forested mountainside where the only movement is a band of rock apes maneuvering along a ridge line. Jumble of triple-canopy covered hills where the only eyes on you are Montagnard Tribesmen crouched motionlessly up slope from a trail, cradling ancient rifles or crossbows.

They're small, thin but wiry with shocks of untamed black hair and ragged shorts, shirts that are a mix of black pajama, old uniforms or none at all. They're figures in a offbeat painting. Ghostly brown shadows rooted in a murky landscape under a ceiling draped in solid green layers. They're hill people, nomads. They don't like the NVA, who force them into slave labor, humping ammo or digging bunkers.

The South Vietnamese treat them like dirt. These

tribesmen are going to lead us through the mountains for awhile.

A smokey ray of light wedges its way to the ground and brightens the ropy thigh of a hunkered-down kid who looks 11 years old. A future chief if he doesn't get caught in a shit storm of our own 500 and 750 pound bombs. The dim light swirls with rumors. Three regiments of NVA swarm the next hill; the Paris Peace Accords are underway; we'll be home by Christmas.

Mountain sides abruptly drop into canyons where clear water hurls over high rock walls into prehistoric pools of deep blue-green warmth. It looks undiluted by special agents, chemicals that are orange but turn brush a sticky purple before killing it. The pool is bliss, a first in a 60-day span of sweat-soaked days and nights burrowed in the dirt. It's playtime, a few carefree moments. Shots ring out. Our radioman, soaking his feet, can't swim. Rounds skip through the water and ricochet off rock as he screams into the handset,

"Cease fire cease fire goddamit.It's us down here. Friendlies goddamit."

A short chopper ride from the kill-me-please mountains. We're in lush jungle, some thick, some thin, and quiet deserted beaches on the coast. Endless unmarred stretches of warm, soft sugar snow.

Days go by. We get better at our jobs, at protecting our brothers, at tight-roping the edge. The blood-letting rite of passage happens at point. It happens early in my fuckin'-new-guy days. The terrain has leveled a little, the brush isn't so dense. The grass is green, waist high in the clearings, ankle high amongst the trees and brushy areas and not so razor-sharp, yet. Clumps of low trees open into small clearings and close off again. I go slow, stepping cautiously. I used a small twig to gently sweep just above ground level to feel for trip wires.

When the NVA hit and cut and run, they leave stragglers to hit the front of the column, slow it down. New guys walk point. I'm doing it by the book. My squad leader, an impatient, hen-house cracker from Alabama comes blowing past everybody, brushes me aside with a harried, "you're going too slow," and walks right into a burst from an AK-47.

I hit the deck and fire a magazine. Everybody toward the front of the column fires up the area. I can hear my squad leader screaming. I crawl up in the tall grass and come to his outstretched hand. He's on his back. His hand is covered in blood so I start wrapping a battle dressing around it. Then I notice his arm is dangling from his shoulder by a shred.

Rounds are flying over us both ways. I gather him up, roll him onto my torso and kind of side-stroke slither us back toward the guys who had come up on line. I remember being pissed that he is screaming all the way. I want him to be quiet, as if the NVA hear us with all the shooting. Back inside our line he's grunting in his nasal twang for morphine. He's been zippered up his left rib cage. The shooting stops and the corpsman is on his way up the column. I didn't know how to comfort my squad leader, so I say something stupid like, "the pain's good for you, it'll make you tough."

I think I've done a good job trying to stop the bleeding and getting him back, but one of his buddies doesn't like my callous remark. He's another cracker, a team leader who becomes our new squad leader. He's the one who, weeks later, takes me aside for a heart-to-heart about not reading so much, being one of the guys.

I tire quickly of all the banter, the put-downs about each other's mother wearing combat boots and driving beer trucks, or how one of them gave your mother $20 so she could get off her back.

It's being in the shit too many times. It triggers a no-time-delay fuse. Hair trigger. I see, hear, feel movement and fire it up, no more catch in my breath. My heartbeat doesn't buck and race. The playground is brutal, but I'm in the game, ready to play. This must have been where I first found myself standing at the threshold. I quit coveting a rear-echelon job, no longer care about being denied R&R time after time. I stop counting the days. It's when I cheapen my own life. It's not a death wish; it just doesn't matter. There's little to remind me of some other world. Death and dying is all around. I deal.

I know a Vietnamese woman who survived an air strike on her village; who worked as a prostitute, unbeknownst to her mother, to support her family; who endured racial hatred, beatings, rape by Vietnamese troops because she fucked Americans; who survived war as a young teenager.

She told me something her mother told her when she was very young on the way to Cho Lon Market one morning, where she and her younger sister sold tea at the Cho Lon bus stops all day. She was seven. Her mother told her not to dream of being a rich business owner; there was too much corruption now. Not to wish to be a princess; it was too much work to stay in favor, to be the number one wife. Not to wish to be a star in heaven; it would be too lonely. Her mother told her to be a riverbank. No matter what the river brings – leaves from a beautiful tree, litter from upstream, fish that rest under a root along the bank, floods that tear away the bank, clear water that polishes the stones along the riverbank. Whatever comes to the riverbank, whatever happens to it, the riverbank accommodates it. Live your life like the riverbank, whatever comes along, deal with it.

Our lives changed courses and our inner selves eroded and flattened out. We might suffer or prosper near it, but we don't battle the river. We deal with what is lef – sometimes a wide murky bog, sometimes a steep slippery slope, sometimes a bank of serenity.

My whole existence is simplified. We try to keep each other alive a little longer. Survival is a lesser issue; it's automatic. Experience and instincts handle it. After too many wake-ups in the bush something else emerges. Now getting some is the thing. I start grooving on the excitement and challenge in the killing zone. I pick up the scent of the pure sex. Darkness.

The killing around me, the killing I do, the willingness to have my meat on the line day after day jazzes me up. Fucks me up. I want a fight.

But here's the price I, as an adrenalin junkie, pay – a darkened soul, a deadened heart. The arm of my emotional radar doesn't sweep any more. The blips are gone. Love, hope, goals, dreams. My passion is twisted. Home is where? It's right here man, Nam au Go Go, where the action is.

I'm just another adrenalin-addled kid sucked into the dark night. The bitch goddess seduces us like a foxy older lady getting a boy to go fetch. Here boy, get some.

Wending my way through the incomprehensible

underworld of killing shifts instincts like a sudden rain. I start out hot, exhausted, fearful for days and days. Somewhere I cross the line and I'm cool under fire. I'm cold about life. Guys have it, then they don't. On or off, simple as a light switch. The world is a dangerous place. This is where the action is.

Which world is real? Chasing the American dream or living with your meat on the line day and night. We're young kids riding a spiraling descent into a world of no taboo and no restraint. Just survive.

I end up with a team out on its own – no supervision to mess up, no ops planned from a desk. Bottom-up management in 1968. We run things and the backseat brass spiff up their records. All over Viet Nam 18- to- 21-year-olds were figuring out how to operate in a strange country against an enemy with decades of guerrilla warfare experience and a cause, to boot.

When was the last time Americans fought this kind of war? We have to figure out how to protect civilians and fight around them. How to guess who is who. How to win the hearts and minds of people who are terrorized by their own kind, if they cooperate with us; we have to move people from a small fishing hamlet in a free-fire zone to a ville in a secure area while being harassed by fire from NVA troops; we have to arrange to have supplies flown in that they'll need to start life anew.

We do this. Three nineteen-year-olds in the bush with a radio. Coordinating psy-ops (psychological operations) leaflet drops, talking to civilians in a hostile area about a better chance to survive, getting a village chief to buy into accommodating a slew of new families. How to keep the upper hand in a hot area with civilians caught in the middle, while rear-eschelon pogues resent that we operate as a rogue outfit. They sit around drawing lines on maps.

We don't need them to contact army psy-ops, or the Red Cross or Vietnamese honchos. We don't need them. They aren't going to come rushing out as a reaction force when we get in a hum. We don't call them before we make a move. We call the army for medevacs and gun-ships. We call Jake, the Air force spotter pilot in a prop plane, to get in the air over us in minutes with jets on the way. The Navy Swift Boat uses us as a checkpoint and backs us up with firepower, supplies us with steak and strawberries. We network, form alliances, partnerships.

But then, how to use it when you've got it just a radio call away. Here's the call sign for *The New Jersey.* One round has the heft of a pick up. The kill radius is huge. I'm afraid to call it in.

The power is immense. Call in artillery, gun-ships, Cobras, Phantoms, Puff, a C-130 plane that is a flying platform for 20 mm cannons that could cover a football field in solid lead in seven seconds. Our corpsman dispenses medical aid to villagers and medevacs kids with raging fevers, along with their moms. We try to show the Vietnamese troops how to kick ass. Win those hearts and minds.

Chapter 19
On the Job Training

If I make it home I can go to school, but not on the GI Bill. A flat $130-a-month wouldn't go far toward a college education. I could enter a management trainee program. How about meetings to plan a meeting? Later I can take direction from someone ten years my junior who's never been out of his own backyard. Will it be easy to work alongside a back stabber? A slacker? Care for a game of office politics?

All that life and death decision making with the clock ticking; all that split-second thinking to keep a team from being overrun. Those ops I coordinated or advised on for other branches that discovered we had a hot AO, don't seem to transfer in a work environment oozing with fragile egos and petty turf protecting.

Viet Nam produced guys who previously had been overlooked, underestimated, or who never had an opportunity for rising to the occasion. Thousands of on-the-ground trained leaders in their early twenties came back to a world that was indifferent about Viet Nam, that operated as if there were no war, that wondered why someone would care about the welfare of people affected by workplace decisions, by business decisions.

Thousands came home who were mission-oriented, knew the value of teamwork, who were willing to go under, over and around meaningless roadblocks. Step on some toes, get the job done. If you can't handle being mired down by process, fuck it; it don't mean shit. Cut and run before you get pushed out. Again and again. Process when you're used to production. Gamesmanship when you're used to fighting.

On-the-job training in the bush is the best training for survival in situations I'll never see again. My senses sharpen like razor wire: A new radar emerges. I feel a person's presence without sight or sound. Walking point in no man's land and steering a course with my gut. It's about reacting just right time after time. They hit, you hit back. A shadowy curve in a tree line is a perfect place for an ambush. Once or twice I could feel them waiting. Slip around their flank and throw a grenade. No telltale muzzle flash to trace back. The tree line erupts with automatic fire and we're way outnumbered. Sometimes we slip away and call in artillery and wait for first light to see what's what, and sometimes we flat out run for it.

Why did I crouch just as a round ripped head high the tree I was leaning on? Maybe it's luck. Maybe it was a gut thing. A dud mortar round slams me with mud as I fill my squad's canteens at a trickle of water. Rounds zip my pants pocket, kick sand between my feet. I get caught in the open when a rocket attack crashes in. Slabs of flying steel boom off the ground, shear off trees. Can I outrun a screaming box car hurtling from the sky?

Close calls become thrilling –escaping death again. A bit later, my body is shaking hard, my autonomic brain trying to cope. The excitement is addictive – synapses firing full auto, epinephrine surging. I feel so cool under fire. I'm fast; I'm bad. Throw a grenade. Cut and run. Mock them. My guile seeds a little notoriety; my luck becomes an issue. A little more twisting, a little more risk taking. I'm unaware of where I'm headed.

Chapter 20
Marijuana Experiment

Unnoticed, two NVA soldiers crest the little rise on the narrow trail. Just as I point to show one of my guys where to keep an eye out they come around a slight bend in the narrow trail. And nearly bump into us.

"Oh my god," Barr gasps as he stood next to me on the trail.

The eyes on both the enemy soldiers pop wide. They wheel and take off.

This happens during an experiment – getting high before we go on patrol. We blow a chance at capturing two NVA in full uniform. Ooten may have wounded one. We find a little blood on the trail. All of our excursions into this area are strictly hit and run, since we are always so outnumbered. We have to get out of here and head back to our compound. Everyone is dogged by the blown opportunity.

The joints come sealed in clear packets of 10 and each joint is about five inches long. Some are treated with opium. We get them occasionally, when one of us gets to a rear area. We had two ways to unwind – swimming in the ocean and smoking a joint. We save them for bright nights when we are too visible to go sneaking and peeking. We gather in my bunker. This is before Jameson comes out to six.

On the nights we unwind, smoking, eating and listening to rock 'n' roll on Armed Forces Radio, we let the Biet Laps stand guard for us. One stands watch on our bunker. On clear nights the sand gleams. The sky looks like spilled salt spread on a bright black piece of marble. The black line of the ocean sparkles where the phosphorous tumbles in the breaking waves.

The joint, we call them telephone poles, goes around and around the bunker, four of us seeing who can take the biggest drag. The clouds billow and the laughter starts. Singing and laughing, getting nice. We lie in hammocks. We are tripping. When we get the munchies we open a new case of C-rations and everyone digs in for their favorite meals. The best part is the coffee and cigarettes after. We think menthol holds a high, so it's really a treat when someone gets a carton of stateside Kools.

We mix every packet of cocoa and coffee and cream and sugar of a two-day supply from a meal into a juice can of water. I concoct a double tall mocha 20 years before Starbucks hits Seattle. The first time I drink an espresso in the early 90's I'm launched back to that bunker on those rock 'n' roll starry nights.

We wait for a dark night for our experiment. The four of us smoke at about 3 a.m., saddle up and leave the wire. We go further up the beach, but just short of the bunkers where we keep making contact. We follow a narrow trail from the beach into the jungle to where a slight rise levels out. We sit on the trail, two of us facing south and two facing north. By 9 a.m. it must be 85 degrees.

We are nodding in the warm sun on a trail we've never been on. Ooten and Arnold are sitting side by side facing Barr and me. We're standing side-by-side across from them. The high has worn off. I feel like I could melt into the sand. My rifle is leaning on a bush across from me and next to Arnold. We're this little tired group on a narrow trail, and I know we should be spread out and watching.

I'd been watching the area in front of me in a similar setting, back at 1-1-7 when we stopped to take a break on a bright morning like this. When the grenade went off I saw the flash of movement and fired at a fleeing Viet Cong. One KIA. I'd been watching the whole time when we inserted by boat up here another time and moved into the tree line in darkness. I caught the blur of movement in the night and fired, wounding a fleeing enemy soldier on watch.

Now we were north of our position again in a hot area grouped up and sleepy.

"Okay, we have to spread out a little and watch the trail. Ooten, go down a bit and watch that way. Arnold, go down a bit and watch this way," I said pointing.

"Oh my god," Barr whispers in amazement.

Arnold, who is sitting down, facing me, opens up. I can't reach for my 16 without getting my arm shot off. I take off chasing them. I light out after them and Barr is on my heels. The trail drops down a rise, so we are out of the line of Arnold's fire. Ooten starts blooping out M-79 rounds that arc into the area where the chase is on. We have to pull up.

The two were walking side-by-side practically touching on the narrow trail and one pawed at the other trying to get turned around and the hell out of there.

They walked right up on us and caught us off guard. And they made their bird, skyed up. Gone, to live another day. It was their lucky day. It was crazy. I hope those two made it to the duration, and can tell about their close call.

Chapter 21
Buzzed by Phantoms

Nothing is as startling as an F-4 buzzing you as you're walking on a beach.

It was quiet time, a day off. We'd gone down to Ky Phu ville to get haircuts and visit with the people. It was unusual for the whole team to be in the ville at the same time. The sky was a blazing blue, the ocean blue and rolling along. A quiet stillness seemed to magnify the vast expanse of deserted beach framed by the tree line and the long white curls of the breaking surf. Hot sun on a pristine blanket of sugar sand.

We're walking single file, the only way that feels comfortable—slightly spread out, slightly staggered. Ky Phu is six or seven klicks south of our position. Between the ville and our pos is uninhabited jungle. We are just ambling along, each of us lost in our own thoughts—an easy walk on a beautiful morning. It's hard to conceive the term "serenity" in a war, but that's the picture on that morning.

The surf slides in so softly you could barely hear the water. We never see them coming. The jets are on the deck and must have been for quite a ways behind us. They fly by just five feet above the water and and 10 feet out from the beach. I feel something, before I see it out of the corner of my eye and hit the beach. I see the pilot of the second craft grinning.

Two jets in single file sneak up on us, thunder the beach and climb straight up in tight spirals. Silver F-4 Phantoms streaking along the ground, a spectacular little prank – Marine Air giving the grunts a little thrill. When our eyes pop back in our heads we laugh our asses off.

I didn't get an R&R for 12 months, and when I did I spend four days pretty much wired, freaked out in Sydney. I didn't do the usual thing – get a room and girl and drink and fuck. I avoid the scene, the whole area and never even have a drink. I get laid once by an American ex-pat, the sister of a girl I knew in high school. I'd heard she was in Sydney and looked her up. I would see her at a friend's house a couple years after I got out and we acted like it had never happened.

In Sydney I'm wired and don't sleep much. It's just such a shock after nearly a year in the bush. My world goes topsy-turvy. I don't realize I'm in a state of extreme anxiety. One night I slip into the surf off the rocks on Bondi Beach. I swim out in the darkness until I bump into the shark nets. Heavy hemp mesh. I have a difficult time getting back on the beach in the heavy surf and jagged rocks.

I meet an East German girl who escaped over the Berlin Wall. She is a ballerina with long blond hair. I watch her work out in her tights. I have about 50 pictures of her. She takes me to the zoo, where I hold a Koala Bear. She takes me to the art museum, where I think I've discovered some new insight into life and a new understanding of what is going on in a painter's head. Things seem to have a profound effect on me. I think I was in a state of shock or something.

At 1-1-6 our team swam in the ocean when we could. I learned to body surf in warm, clear water. The phosphorous gleamed ghostly swirls when we swam at night. Just for a few moments we didn't feel the killing all around us, all in us. When we laughed it wasn't black humor; it was innocent, joyful.

Guys in the rear had good times. They had booze and weed just about any time they wanted it. They had movies, shows with Philippine or Thai bands that could cover a song better than any American band, and they had girl musicians, saucy little nymphs to die for.

If you got near a rear area, there were young girls with sleek bodies who took you to a little room behind a curtain. Some were sprite, some were somber. Most of them helped support their parents and siblings. Military propaganda warned that Viet Cong prostitutes infiltrated these areas and wore razor blades up their vaginas. Nobody bought that. They also warned that Viet Nam was rampant with Black Syphilis. It ate all your organs and you died a slow death. There was no treatment for Black Syphilis, so if you caught it you were quarantined on an island off Japan until you died.

When you're in the bush, you figure your chances aren't that good, and you worry about Black Syph for about five seconds while a bright-eyed young thing with perfect skin, shiny hair and firm little body tugs at your buttons, chirping, "me love you too much." There's not much opportunity when you spend your tour in the boonies, and you didn't think about sex that much. Daydreams were about food. But I still cherish the few times that beautiful young girls made me feel wonderful.

I'm in Tam Ky once at the Army base looking for a ride to our Chu Lai headquarters and bump into an Air Force spotter pilot at the mess hall. I tell him about our team and how much contact we make.

"Why don't you go up with me tomorrow?"

In the little two-seater O-3 Cessna, I strap on the Buck Rogers helmet with visor and mike and follow along as he explains how to flip a switch on the dash to cut in on radio traffic to talk to him. From the air I see all the colors of the jungle, light green to dark green and the red dirt. I see the cleared land with perfect squares of emerald-green rice surrounded by dikes and canals.

I see the sharp contrast between the ground, the foliage and the blue ocean. It's a bright serene morning, and he teaches me to fly the plane. I radio my guys as we fly over 1-1-6. The swift boat is off our pos and I radio them and tell them what's up. On a map I point to the area north of our pos where we'd been getting regular contact. The show is about to begin.

Jake, the call sign Wallace the pilot uses, calls in an air strike and a pair of Phantoms out of Da Nang Air base shows in about five minutes and start circling overhead, little specks in the sky above us.

"Hold on."

He flips the plane 90 degrees and points it straight at the ground and fires a white phosphorous marker round. A white plume raises straight up and the first jet screams down, levels out, drops a 250 pound high explosive bomb and climbs straight up. The second jet takes the same run. We're flying a tight circle over the target and Jake adjusts their hits and they start their second run. Armed forces rock 'n' roll is playing on our net. As the second run starts Jake gets a call.

"Jake Oh 3, this is Foxtrot Mike Mike one niner. Interrogative, we heard you have targets. Can we come down?"

In a minute, another pair of phantoms show up and

circle above the first two and wait their turn. More secondary explosions fill the air with black smoke.

"Jake Oh 3, this Lima Oscar one one. Ah, we have no targets and are over the big blue to drop our load. Can we hit for you?"

"Lima Oscar one one, Roger that. We are over X-ray 84427-niner."

Three pairs of jets are stacked liked saucers over the target. We still fly tight circles right over the target and captain Wallace is adjusting their hits. The air at our level fills with black smoke.

Mick Jagger is wailing, "I can't get no, no satisfaction."

Wallace breaks in on the intercom.

"Hey, can you see where those jets are?"

A phantom streaks by our windshield 10 yards directly in front.

"Oh, there they are," he says.

My heart is pumping and the rock 'n' roll back drop is making me giddy. Jets are making their runs, secondary explosions fill the sky, we keep flying right over the target and the Stones keep rockin'. It is just wild. I'm definitely jacked up.

The first four jets say "adios" and the last two have made two runs. Then they spot the swift boat.

"Charlie Leader, I see our Navy boys down there."

"Roger, Charlie One, why don't we go down and say hello."

"Roger that, I'll take 'em on the left, you take them on the right."

The phantoms tip and scream down out of the sky.

"Leader, this One. I got you a little overshot, here."

"Roger, one. Let's cross."

They scream down, cross and swoop up on both sides of the 50 foot boat. It's rocking like crazy as the phantoms spiral straight up into the bright blue.

Chapter 22
I Know Luck

I've heard that some psychologists say that there is no such thing as luck. Combat made me a firm believer in luck.

Guys were killed the day before they left the bush to go on R&R. Just one more day of luck and they would have been fucking their brains out instead of never having another chance at the pleasure boys joke about dying for. I once heard an interview on National Public Radio where a psychologist said the world is about sex.

Even when you've tasted the sweet essence of luck, I know there's no guarantee. I don't feel a guardian angel on my shoulder. After awhile I didn't see guys praying to make it. They're making sure their luck icons are on them before they go on ambush or start the day's hump. I know it's a requirement for survival. When rounds go through my pants pocket or kick up dirt between my feet, how can I say their aim is off? No, their aim is good. And so was my luck.

I believed I could borrow luck from my main partner. I believed while we were together, our luck could be shared. But I never believed I had a guarantee that I would always be lucky. When it was there it was there. When it wasn't, your chances of survival dropped. No mystery. I don't think it's a state of mind, or some reward. It's some mysterious force, or maybe it's a crapshoot.

My number comes up on a day that is perfect for getting wasted. The trail widens where a couple of bunkers are in the middle of nowhere. There are no villages around.

The bunkers are for fighting, or for ducking artillery or for storing ammunition. The day is bright, a bright day in jungle that they can easily slip quietly through if they are stalking somebody. The Truong Giang River flows on one side of the narrow strip of land and the South China Sea rolls up on the other.

One of the bunkers looks sturdy and sinister. It's a smooth shaped mound of sand, an upside-down bowl on the edge of a forty-foot clearing along a jungle trail north of our compound. I decide to blow it.

I load my pockets with blocks of C-4 plastic explosive, some timing fuse and blasting caps, and squeeze through the opening. My team gets in the tree line behind the bunker to cover the clearing in front of the entrance. I'm the right size for tunnels, still it's a snug fit as I drop down a level, come to a turn, go a little further, turn and drop down to another level. The walls are lined with the large masonry blocks that are used for crematoriums by the Cham, an indigenous tribe.

At the end of the six-foot long bottom level I pack C-4 into the corners where the walls meet the timbered ceiling. I have a blasting cap on about a 20-second fuse jammed into the upper charge. I light the fuse and try to turn around but it's too tight. I have to back out. Crawling backward and going up a level means slithering up a vertical wall feet first.

Back, up, turn; back, up, turn. Scraping up and out, I wheel and bolt through the clearing because it's faster than getting around the bunker into the tree line. At a dead run I glimpse a green figure dead ahead and I hit the ground as I hear the roar of an AK-47. I'm like spit on a griddle. There is a blank time, a period of time I have no recollection of. Barr said I was on my feet bumping into trees, my eyes huge, going "He missed me, he missed me."

We backtracked him to a spider hole along the bank of the river.

"Drop a grenade in and let's go." I'm too spooked to fuck with this.

We stop at the site on the way back. The bunker is intact as far as I can tell. The others pick up the 30 shell casings about 20 feet from where I had been flopping like a fish out of water.

"You should make a belt out of these," laughs Barr. "You must have freaked him running right at him."

I think I'm fucking lucky.

Chapter 23
The Price You Pay

What was that image of soldiering back on the block, on main street, on campus? *Defending your country from Communism.* Yeah sure. Fulfilling your obligation? Fool. Keeping your honor intact. Really? Being a war hero? No matter. Survivors who make it home don't get close to anybody. No intimacy – just keep feelings at arm's length year after year.

Things could blow up anytime, fall apart any minute. The unknowing seem witless, that civilian, mundane joy obnoxious, their dreams pointless. Could I hide my special knowledge, my contempt for fucked up leadership? Could I control that volatile prolonged arousal when it's lit off?

I bury my combat experience deep in my mind, roll out the concertina wire, set up the claymores and add layer after layer of sandbags and camouflage to keep the secrets. My pos is impenetrable.

Kids have no inkling about the cost of surviving combat at twenty. That comes later with payments due for five, ten, twenty, thirty years. Pay up or fold. Many check out. The concept of death is not a strange one. It seems inevitable at times, a bargain at times.

At twenty the main issue was the will to live. Somewhere along the way to Khe Sanh, I decide to survive. Now fear of dying becomes passe. I realize feelings will crack me and learn to shut down. Then I become a student of the game. That's when I find I'm on a lurid trail and know something is changed. I live in the moment – food, water, ammo, action, a dry place to hunker down. A poncho or hole in the ground is home. It's home. And if the night is clear, I'm staying in a thousand-star hotel. A warm breeze and the surf murmuring a lullaby. My street of dreams is a bunker with a hammock. The roof doesn't leak. A good neighborhood is out in the bush, away from a firebase and rats, two-legged as well as four.

Life without a daily barrage of incoming is good. No FNGs to worry about. Forget hot chow. There are no garbage details. There are no busybody neighbors, or military lifers, just tight friends, bush rats whose goal in life is just that – theirs and yours.

My career is surviving and work is challenging. Very exciting – criss-crossing the line between life and death. Escaping death, that's the big deal you closed. Sitting together in a bunker and laughing about close calls, saluting Charles for having the balls to nearly fire-up your ass. Laughing, trembling and shaking down the adrenalin. Eating all the fruit cocktail, peaches and pound cake out of a case of C's. That's our promotion celebration, our employee of the year bonus. We're alive and living large.

I slipped into the smoky haze of combat and liked it there. After a while the big picture is clear – there is death out there; there is death in you. Get in there and deal. Be a riverbank. Go with the flow. Keep your wits, your weapons switched on, everything ready to get cookin'. Everything you need is handy – a weapon, a radio, a map.

There isn't any tollbooth at the bridge to this madness, but it's on every trail. Soldiers pay each time they saddle up for a patrol, every time they set up an ambush. Every time they drag the body of a friend to a dust-off chopper. When they fire at a shadow and find a kid wide-eyed and riddled and dying. I stop giving any of it a thought. I don't register it. But I can't walk away from it forever. I bury it, and it's part of me.

We keep searching for more thrill. Our area of operation is everything on this spit of land ahead of us. We patrol and lay in ambush. We hunt around the clock, then take an occasional break. Dip in a slow river, the water warm, flat and murky. The banks are overgrown, darkening patches of water. One disappears in it. Eyeballs floating on liquid slate.

Swim in the warm ocean. The beach is pristine and deserted—our private shangri-La. The water is a shade of chloride toothpaste and clear as an Olympic aqua training center. Soothing warm in the swells, like a heating pad on low. The surf churns like an Easlen spa at Big Sur. Share a joint, a rare pure letdown. Getting nice. Passing around a telephone pole, a ready-made joint six inches long and round as a young girl's pinkie. It's potent but not wicked. No bite. Wire a dead radio battery to a transistor radio, just enough juice for some sounds. Motown. Martha and the Vandellas, "Dancin' in the Street", R&B, Otis Redding, ("Sittin' on the) Dock of the Bay."

"Geez I wish they'd play Country Joe and the Fish."

"Aw man, you know Armed Services Radio won't play no protest songs."

"Fuck, I would, man. What would they do? Bust me and send me to the bush?"

"Hey, hey, if I fuckin' nod here and they play This Magic Moment...," they already know what I want.

"Yeah, yeah, ... wake you up."

"Or 'Runaway'" by Del Shannon.

One night, getting nice, the instrumental "The Horse" pulls us to our feet. Four guys bend over at the waist trying to coordinate jive moves. Grunt choreography. We howl. And then the jokes:

Arnold stands.

"Dig it man, There's a couple brothers in this squad that's on patrol. And a sniper pops a round. And the squad leader yells, 'get down.' And the brothers start doin' the boogalu."

He's gyrating and pumping his arms.

Smitty, who is black, throws his head back and cackles and hoo, hoos, laughing his ass off.

"Man, you chucks (white men) can't dance, no fuckin' way. You ain't born black, you ain't got soul."

A cozy starlit night, a bright night is made for relaxing, not for sneaking and peeping. Just right for joking, feeling off guard, turning on. "Whoosh, wooosshh!" A small-town kid tries his first joint. High on laughing, the rock and roll lifts you up. All of us digging that wooosh. A lovely way to feel, to feel something. Feel nice. Who's monitoring the radio? Doc. Okay man, no sweat. Take another hit. Maybe it will let you sleep.

I write this and I think, would getting laid have put us over the top? Strange we didn't think about sex, seldom talked about it. Combat, the violence builds into an erotic tension. The danger jacks you up and it is like sex, in that once a young man gets there, he wants it all the time. The violence is a substitute for sex; my yearning for pleasure for sexual gratification, has been replaced by a new rush, a more powerful excitement, and it is real.

Killing becomes erotic. Death too. So after awhile, the sexual stimulus had to be therein – my presence, my face to her face. The goddess of war luring me on. This is what she does. Direct stimulus. Live or die. The sexual fantasy spark is snuffed. When I wanted to get some I wanted a fight, my meat on the line. I realized that sex wasn't in my head every three seconds anymore. I figured, well, we've got no hookers out here in the bush, we've got no USO babes on a stage. But there's an urge, a powerful need.

Chapter 24
A Gentle World

My sex drive didn't dim; it shifted. 1966 and '67 were prior to the sexual revolution, and I'd only been laid a few times before going into the military. In Viet Nam I worried I might be killed before I got more of the uppermost thing on my mind. Before going over, I tried to talk Linda Springs, who I barely knew, into giving me a memorable send off.

"This could be maybe my last chance," I said. "I could be killed over there."

It didn't work.

I got laid a couple more times in Viet Nam, but not before I'd spent five months in the bush. When I got transferred into Combined Action Group and the small teams, I was sent to the Marine base in Da Nang for orientation. I was walking to the base from where I'd been dropped off from the LZ. As I approached the perimeter of the base on China Beach, a boy of about 10 asked me, "Hey Marine. You want boom boom?"

"Yeah." I even had money. When I processed out of the infantry in Phu Bai, I got paid. I had some cash for about the first time in Viet Nam. "Come with me," the boy said, and he took me to his home, a shack near the base. His sister was there, about 17 years old, quiet and very pregnant. She laid down on the low wood bed and slipped off her silk bottoms. I sweated over her for a few minutes and part of the satisfaction was ridding myself of the thought in the back of my mind since I'd been in country that my sex life had been curtailed and that I could die before it ever resumed again. It was my first time since I'd been in the military. Other than that it was all almost somber. My first experience with a hooker and I felt not just pleasure, but a sense of relief. I mean it wasn't the best, but at 19 there is no such thing as bad sex. At least I wouldn't die in a foreign land without getting laid at least once.

There were a couple of other times with women just as young, but pretty and lively. And I could be a giver, not a taker, not a destroyer. They would be the highlight of my tour.

Once I had crossed the threshold into the dark night my passion wasn't for fucking. I got caught up in the ecstasy of combat, revved by the thrill of living at the edge of death, of escaping death, sexual energy took on a new form – putting my meat on the line and seeing if I could escape death again. A fire fight *is* sexual. Killing became seductive.

My goddess's allure became irresistible as I slipped through moist tangles in the pitch black jungle to rendezvous with her. The warm fine sand I pressed flat against lying in ambush were her silky thighs. I opened my pants and ground into her during the long wait for rebels to glide down a trail into my sight picture. The jungle sighed and it was her moan whipping up my urge until I could shoot.

The corpse of a Viet Cong teenager was more than a dead woman in this world of no taboo. She was a beautiful, slender lover lying quietly in a single layer of black silk. Was she a gift from my dark angel for my prowess, for my devotion to her guile? I was a toy in the hands of this dark temptress who had lured soldiers into unspeakable adventure and thrill since the beginnings of war.

There were no camp followers in the bush. You could never have the young beauty in a hamlet who may glimpse your way in curiosity. She knew what you were and what you did.

So my drive shifted to the thrill of hunting and being hunted by other men, and even women. The memory of the Viet Cong teenager who threw a grenade as we paused on patrol still makes me shiver. She had this desire to kill. This beautiful, young woman had not tried to kill in fear, but in lust. It was the kind of lust I knew.

It's life at its fullest, at its highest degree when it could end at any second any day or night. When I discovered this fleeing killer was a beautiful girl, I wanted her. I wanted to feel her smooth, still-warm silk.

I wasn't thinking of sex when I found myself in a frontier boom town toward a rear area.

A Vietnamese kid who knew opportunity took me to a storefront on a dusty street. It was a family's home and business, and the father smiled when I greeted him in Vietnamese. His daughter, so young and exquisite. It was like a dream when she leaned into my arm and teased with a smile. I sensed no tawdry feeling as her mother tended a small cooking fire and we slipped behind a curtain at the back. This was war and there is no taboo.

She arches as I slip my arm around her slender back and she whispers in my ear, "You good man. You good man, John." Her soothing heat glows from sparkling eyes and silky skin, and she loves me in a caring way.

I still thank the heavenly girl who took me to a gentle world on a giving afternoon.

Chapter 25
The Goddess

We must have been asexual in the bush. Yeah, I figure it out. Get back to a rear area where some teenage slip of a of Suzy Wong flirts or teases and I'm good to go. Out here, no stimulus, not horny. But we are trying to score all right. In and out. Find them, fuck with them and flee with your ass intact and your mind tripping.

The turn on comes with guns roaring. Daring death. But the comparison with flirtation ends here. And then it goes beyond flirtation. We take. We give. We cruise all day, hang out in the shadows all night. Get some. Just like guys back in the world, trying to get some sex. When I spot movement, I feel the tingling starting to build, the urge, the striving to get there. Going for it – hey baby, gimme some. That fucking goddess has her nails in my back, her arm tight around my neck, fingers grabbing hair, yanking my head down.

Shadows come slinking down the trail. The night air is hot. You're in your girlfriend's parents' living room ready to explode, holding your breath, straining for just a little bit more sight picture of a figure carrying an AK-47, then shooting a jet of .223 caliber out your barrel in a zing of thrill churning your balls, every fiber in your nervous system jolted by adrenalin and capped with dopamine. Supercharged ecstasy. Got some action that night. It's Friday night every night on a hot trail. M-16's and AK-47's booming a battle of the bands while the goddess is tonguing my ear, tugging at my buttons.

Did I stop breathing there a split second? This is

freakier than car doors in the driveway and pulling on the wrong pair of pants. That is a burst from the AK that dude just swung down on me. It's not little sister walking in on me and Baby Sue – it's an RPG (rocket propelled grenade) whooshing by my head, taking out the tree up-slope and two Marines behind it. This is not a tease – this svelte, teenage, sweet thing flinging a grenade my way. That bitch tried to do me. A 20-second fire fight is sex, pure sex to us who are hooked. Coming like a hound dog. Chasing an NVA through a tree line like a kid chasing a catch-me-fuck-me tart up the stairs of a frat house. Oh yeah, yeah. Get some.

Pure pussy.

Chapter 26
Jody

I didn't realize it. I never thought it would happen – Jody would be wooing my girlfriend before I even got overseas. Jody is the guy who is fucking girlfriends and wives while husbands and boyfriends are busy in a war.

It wasn't a big shock. I found out MaryRae was seeing somebody six months before I reported to boot camp.

"I think we should see other people," she explained.

It didn't sink in. This was temporary, some experiment to test our love or to raise my commitment level. I was her first boyfriend, and she was my first girlfriend. This whole thing probably sealed my decision to get this military thing out of the way. It would be like going into the Foreign Legion.

I can't remember when drill instructors warned us about Jody. My dreaminess about coming back a war hero, if I actually went to war, which was doubtful because I would pick a job that wasn't dangerous, as the recruiter promised, wasn't a bona-fide fantasy. MaryRae would miss me. I knew this. She told me after we were supposed to be seeing other people and I'd stop by occasionally to repair and cement our relationship. We rolled around on her parents' sofa with my pants around my knees and one leg of hers shucked and out of the way.

"Why are we doing this if you say you don't want to get back together?" I asked.

"Don't you see? I can't resist you."

There was hope. I dropped the idea of becoming a

hero after reading about what was going on over there and about how the Marines were taking 80 percent casualties. Forget the war hero bit, I was going for a safe MOS (military occupation designation) in a safe place. Being in a motor pool in Hawaii would be my top choice.

Up in the Co Roc and Truong Son Mountains I think about MaryRae as a way to distract myself from the dread of dying. I receive a letter with a newspaper clipping of her wedding. I guess they don't know I still care. I feel somewhat crushed, but not enough to go out in a blaze of glory.

I'm not surprised by the turn of events. Jody is a busy guy. MaryRae's parents got married when they were 18 and 16. Mine got married when they were 27 and 25. Mary Rae and I had different notions about the right age for marriage. I show the clipping to my friend Dick Pauria, who I'd met on the flight to boot camp and met again somewhere in the bush.

"You should wipe your ass with it and send it back."

"Yeah well, it's probably better this way. Now I can stop thinking about her. It's better to be over here with nobody back home."

A month or so later, Dick got a letter from his girlfriend's mother with a clipping. He worried me. I had listened to him talk about how they had met, what a prize she was. I knew that. We were both from the same town and I knew of her family. They had a successful business. She'd been a cheerleader, foxy, popular.

"Did you think you guys would get married?" I asked.

"Yeah."

"Before you went in, did she talk about maybe you and her should see other people."

"Yeah."

"I know how it is."

The Jody-fuck stories were common. Jody quite often turned out to be someone's friend, someone's cousin, someone's brother. Young love does not survive a distance of 15,000 miles for a year, especially during the start of the sexual revolution. Young people made up the groundswell of the anti-war movement. We were part of a very unpopular war. We were doomed.

Even if Jody didn't break up marriages or pending marriages, the war did. The survivors were tainted. Why would a young woman stay married to an alien, someone who had seen too much and done too much and would never know peace?

Later, when I come home I move in with a teammate from the rugby team. Rugby smoothes me out some, and the chicks dig the scene, but I can't get with the program. It's six months before I'm comfortable talking to a girl. I have nothing to talk about.

I'm lying on the couch with my knees drawn up under a blanket. In the bedroom, my roommate is getting Friday night rolling with his girlfriend. He bursts into the room and jumps on the couch, looking me in the eyes.

"Gina wants to know why a good looking guy like you is never with a girl. Really, why do you stay home? Why don't you get out and get some?"

About then I meet Sandy Sandusky. She keeps going to rugby games and parties while her boyfriend is in the army stationed in Korea. She laughs and leans into me in the booth at the old Red Robin Tavern where the team goes drinking after games and practices. The whole gang takes a keg home to her house and the party keeps going. In the early morning the house is empty and she is falling asleep on the couch. I get her a blanket. She smiles and says she's going upstairs.

"I don't want to go home," I tell her.

I follow her up. She didn't say anything, starts to undress in the walk-in closet in the bedroom of the old two-story house she rents with another nurse. I watch her slip into a white, slinky teddy. A slim, curvy nurse. Beautiful and fun. She gets in bed.

"You can sleep here, on this side, or there's a mattress in the spare room."

Her eyes and lips smile. She watches me undress and slip under the covers.

I never tell her why I couldn't touch her, why I left when she finally fell asleep. I couldn't be Jody.

Chapter 27
Girl on Top

In combat, sex somehow gets all mixed up with blood lust. So I may talk about it with the same preoccupation a young guy thinks about it.

My Catholic upbringing, my worrying about MaryRae's reputation had tempered it a bit. But we had experimented our way through the wonderful world of sex.

Now in Viet Nam, I fretted. I would die horny, before I could get to R&R. Rest and Recovery is strictly about getting your brains fucked out in places like Singapore, Taipei or Bangkok. You had to have three months in country before you were eligible for R&R. I went twelve months before I got R&R, and I didn't stay in Asia, I went to Sydney. I went under orders to go, so I chose Sydney in order to bump the First sergeant in headquarters off the flight.

West of Highway One near Tam Ky, I'm with a team I've been with a couple days. We stop by a hut along the road to get a coke, and a saucy, pretty girl grabs my hat and says she'd give it back along with a blow job for five dollars. None of the other guys seem interested in any of this type of activity. I figure it's taboo or something. I still remember that naughty, sexy playfulness about her.

Highway One was the main North-South arterial for South Viet Nam. Just a narrow dirt road with truck-stop-like commerce anywhere near a U.S. base. This was a place that would not have existed but for the presence of a foreign army.

Our team stopped by on our way to the MACV

army base. I can't remember why we were there, but there was another saucy, pretty girl hustling and jiving us. She had short western hair and an attitude. I was definitely intrigued.

"I boom boom you for free," she says dragging me into the small room with the wood platform bed and grass mat.

As soon as I got over her, she stops me.

"I do you." And she rolls me onto my back.

She humps and humps until she's dripping sweat and breathing hard.

"Why you no come?" she asks.

But she keeps going till I turn her over, give her a break. In no time I'm dripping over her and then come. She laughs then and says, "You backup long time fuck."

I want to say she picked me and "souvenired" me because I had blue eyes and because she thought I was handsome, or maybe because I could speak a little Vietnamese. Some of these girls supported their parents and brothers and sisters. Some of their families didn't know where the money came from. I liked that she was fun-loving and warm. I liked that she gave me a memory I could pass the long hours with.

Chapter 28
Cowboy

When one guy from my squad came back from the hospital ship, he showed me his cowboy boots. We were in Khe Sanh waiting for the big battle, the hordes of NVA to come pouring out of the hills.

"You brought your boots back here?"

"Yeah. I stopped by supply at Da Nang air base. I just had to have them."

"What if we move out? Are you going to hump them?"

I'd been fascinated by the cowboy thing. My dad grew up on a ranch his father homesteaded in Montana. I always wondered what my life would have been like if he'd stayed in ranching. I liked Lister already, but when I found out he was a cowboy, I liked him even more. He seemed upbeat. He smiled a lot. Unusual. He was off the ranch in New Mexico.

I'd hear about moving cattle from one field to another. How some would lie in the tall grass of a shallow irrigation ditch and they would find them later by the smell. They were so big they couldn't get back on their feet. They'd starve in the thick grass. Lister said he'd come across some rocking and rocking, their eyes bugged out trying to get up.

I didn't even know he'd been wounded. It was during one of the last firefights we got into before we made it to Khe Sanh. Nobody knew how he got hit, where or how bad. We got hit by a company of NVA early one morning and then mortars and rockets started pouring in.

Most of the casualties had been from the mortars. In the trees you hoped the rounds didn't fall near you. If you were dug in, you hoped they didn't fall on you. They sound like freight trains screaming in. I read another Marine's account of incoming and he described it the same – like freight trains screaming out of the air. That screeching screaming sound is far more terrifying than the explosion. It comes in fast and gets louder until the blast.

They hit near you or they don't. You're waiting for the end, the most awful imaginable death. Loud and horrendous. The worst wounds were from incoming, then land mines. Shredded bone and flesh, traumatic amputations. Rocks, twigs, dirt drilled into the wound along with jagged metal.

"My squad was point, the ones they opened up on. I was running for the tree line when the first round came in. Splib Smitty and Rosie were behind me, both killed. I got hit all in the back with shrapnel, got medevaced straight to the hospital ship," Lister said.

He still had that jaunty look and the smile, like nothing had happened. Just been away for awhile. Nice to be back.

"What's the ship like?"

"Nice, man. Hot chow, white sheets on mattresses this thick."

Smiling he held his hands about six inches apart.

"This one nurse from Boston and I got along real good," he smiled.

"After, I could lay on my side, she'd come in at night, lean over me and jack me off. After awhile she'd hop in bed and we'd fuck like spoons in a drawer."

"Man I can't even believe you were getting laid in

the Nam by a round eye."

"Man she was so sweet, just as sweet as could be."

"What she look like?"

"Nice. Slender, small ass, nice tits, curly hair, blue eyes, about 25-years old. I stayed on that ship for an extra two weeks. She kept putting my records at the bottom of the pile. The doctor would come in and say, 'How we doing? I can't find your chart.'"

"It sucks being back here, huh?"

"Nah. I just put my boots on, when I get a chance, and think about my nurse."

Chapter 29
Boat Lady

She's the only one in town who wears the conical peasant hat, the kind you see on everyone working in the rice paddies or ponds, herding cattle or ducks or hauling loads on a balance pole. I meet her on my second return trip to Viet Nam in 2000. If you've seen any picture of people who live and work in Viet Nam countryside, you've seen them. Woven reed, a perfect circle that rises to a peak. In the movies, they go sailing when the choppers swoop down on villagers working the fields. I can't remember the name for them; I was told, but I didn't write it down.

Women who work outside all wear them. They keep the sun off, and that's important. I don't think it's so much for the heat as it is to keep from getting darker. Check out any Vietnamese movie poster, TV ad, calendar or print ad. If there's a woman in the picture, she's nearly white. White is best. Think Chinese royalty in face paint.

Em is in downtown Hoi An, a town about 15 klicks south of Da Nang, near the outdoor market on the river. You will find her on the corner near the bridge, where tourists come and go – shopping, eating, going to their hotels.

She's a boat lady. She's on the river every day. Lives on the island in the river, get's up at 4:30 am, every single morning, gets the family fed, the kids ready for school, the husband ready for work and poles and paddles the narrow, low-sided skiff to town. She's there at 7 and goes home at dark, unless someone wants to go on the river.

I saw her without her hat once, but not on the river. I was in Hoi An four or five days and I went on the river every day. She'd sit on her haunches and just glide the thing along. Pole or paddle. Every once in-a-while I saw her adjust the black cloth band that snugged under her chin. She'd stretch her jaw just slightly. She had light brown skin and perfect teeth. She was thirty-nine with a wonderful smile. These hats must have a diameter of about 14 inches. You can see a person's face, but not from their eyebrows up. She took the hat off when we got to her house the night she invited me to have dinner with her family. Extended family. She wears her hair shoulder-length in a pony tail. She said a hat lasts about one year.

After dinner she pole-paddled me the half-hour back to Hoi An. Her six year old son came along. He offered his hand as we walked the jungle path in pitch black. He offered his hand as I stepped into their boat. We were the only ones on the river under a full moon.

"If you come back Hoi An with a girl friend, I take you at night." She motioned with her hand up river, all around. "Very romantic," she chuckled.

You could barely hear the paddle dip into the water. A soft tweep, tweep. I sat facing her with the moon at her back. Her son nestled against my leg and took my hand. I can't remember if she wore her hat.

Chapter 30
Flashback

I used to fall back into the war all the time. Certain sounds, certain songs, certain shadows – all the triggers could launch me back to the war. When I came home to Tacoma, Washington in 1969, I couldn't go through a gate without checking for booby traps, couldn't walk side-by-side with people. I came home to my parents' house not far from Fort Lewis Army Base and McChord Air Force Base.

The sound of the fort's air traffic was something. Hueys, Phantoms, C-141 Star Lifters and the big jumbo transports moving troops to Asia. It was the Summer of '69. I'd grown up with the woom, boom of the fort's artillery range. I was used to it. It didn't annoy me. 81 mm mortars, 105 mm and 155 artillery pieces were being fired by guys in training for duty in Viet Nam. But the choppers just took me back, the whump, whump, whump of the rotors.

I still shiver, mist up when I hear Jay and the American's version of "This Magic Moment." Somewhere in Viet Nam I heard it on Armed Forces Radio and something about it grabbed me hard. Other versions suck, but theirs had a majestic, hymnal quality to it. I don't know if it was the lyrics or the sound of it, the crescendos. The hopefulness of the lyrics grabbed me, made me well up. It became my Viet Nam song along with Del Shannon's "Runaway."

I was humping through the Annamitique Mountain Range from the DMZ and into Laos. I'd sing the words I knew softly. A Marine from a different squad used to come to me when we were digging in at night. Or when we moved out in the morning, he'd find me. He was big, but not tall and had dark hair, dark eyes. I can't remember where he's from.

"Sing Runaway," he'd ask.

"I sing like shit, man."

"No. Come on sing it."

"As I walk along, I wonder what went wrong with our love, a love that was so strong. I'm a walkin' in the rain to the border and I feel the pain, wish'n you were here by me, my little runaway, run, run, run runaway.... and I wonder, I won, won wonder where she has gone, an' I wonder where she will stay.... my little runaway."

When I'm by myself and I hear either of these songs come on the radio, I stop what I'm doing. Sometimes I'll even pull to the side of the road and let them wash over me, feel the feeling, let the tears come.

I'm trying to forget the thing, pretend I hadn't been part of it. The anti-war sentiment was strong, and I knew the deal. I should have been leading the marches, closing down the freeway, throwing medals, telling it like it is at rallies. But I need distance from it. I want no part of it.

I'm afraid of physical confrontation. I know if I get started I won't stop till there is a lifeless body at my feet. I definitely can't be around weapons. More than once I reach for my M-16, startled by some noise. One day I'm trying to get two of my horses that had gotten loose from the pasture and are on the road that went by the little farm my brother and I rent. We aren't farming. It isn't really a farm anymore, just a place in the sticks. For a few years I prefer living in the hills. I'm trying to sneak through the pasture, get to the road and cut the horses off. I hadn't gotten to the wire when a pick-up loaded with Indians tries to spook them (the place was on the Muckleshoot Reservation). They are all yelling, the driver blaring the horn, veering to chase them on down the road. I want a weapon so bad. I'm mad. There are no warning shots in me.

I'd worry about that feeling that came over me—wanting a weapon. My temper would redline in an instant, then stay up for hours. In taverns, on construction jobs when someone pissed me off, shoved me on the dance floor, crossed a picket line, I struggled with my urge to kill. If there were no witnesses, it would have been a different story.

I always worried about witnesses and about ending up in jail. How do you handle anger when you've just spent thirteen months in a world without taboo? The things most people worried about seemed pretty inconsequential to me. The thing I worried about – the ease with which killing had become a part of me – was deadly serious.

Years later, the things that triggered anger, like songs, smells, shadows and Hueys, have less and less effect. But I still relive my tour at night. I weep as I lay in bed as memories scroll by, as scenes vividly take me back. The triggers are a ticket to an all night movie. I lie awake all night long, then commute to a construction site, or to some cubicle in a maze on the floor of a state agency. I'd be patrolling, ambushing, ducking artillery and rockets all night long and then go to work. Some nights I'd roam around the house or apartment then lie down and quietly weep. Sometime in the early to mid 80's, I read *Fields of Fire* by James Webb, former Marine infantry platoon leader. For two weeks I relived my tour every night. So I never went to see Oliver Stone's "Platoon."

I read about vet counselors being at theaters to help guys who were blown away by it. Years later I bravely checked out the video. I laughed at the Hollywood attempts to depict the nuances of surviving combat, of getting away from guys you couldn't trust with your life.

You didn't pick fights unless you were going to win, and you sure didn't fight anywhere where weapons were handy like in the movie. I shook my head when I finally saw it, chagrined that I'd bought into the hype about it being too real, too graphic. Too Hollywood is more like it. A chopper abandoning a live dude on the ground. I don't think so.

Because it is based on memoir, the film "When Heaven and Earth Changed Places" is more realistic. I stayed awake for nights after that. Kubrick's "Full Metal Jacket" has a disturbingly real feel to it in some ways. The boot camp scenes are pretty accurate. The sniper picking at a wounded grunt. The murder, or rather execution of the sniper. Rape.

On the bad nights, I'm quiet, stealthy – never disturb girlfriends or my wife or girlfriends later on. One morning I slip downstairs to get the newspaper and to call my nine-year old son at his mother's. I'm standing at the kitchen counter by the phone when I glance at a picture of a father looking over his eleven-year-old boy as he dies on a hospital gurney. I'm launched back to CAP 1-1-7 the morning the dead children were brought to the gate of the compound. In my kitchen, I can hardly stand up. My chest heaves. Convulsions pummel me and I fight to stay on my feet. A dead child on a gurney.

I'd been at CAP 1-1-7 a short time. It was out there, miles from friendlies, accessible only by chopper or the Truong Giang River. Across the river was a small fishing village. On our side of the river any villes nearby had been abandoned. The enemy incoming one night were long, overshot our pos. Well, I think, they don't have this pos dialed in. Roberts had last watch, but he woke everybody when the villagers showed up at our gate.

"Get doc and get to the gate," he called in to the bunker.

Mamma-san and two papa-sans stood quietly above four children lying on army stretchers, jerry-rigged beds they'd probably scavenged from some dump near some large base. The kids' guts and skeletons spill and poke through their shredded skin. It's as if some butcher ran amok flailing at bodies with cleavers and then jumbled up the bone, flesh and organs together and laid them out for viewing.

Dead kids on stretchers. Some more children stand quietly with bloody rags barely covering deep rends in their arms or legs. The kids didn't whimper, didn't make a sound. Their big brown eyes looked up in bewilderment. Mama-san reeled off anguished chatter, her voice rising and falling. I looked from the wounded kids to the dead ones. The sand was warm on my feet. The sun was bright and the Banyan leaves glistened green. The day was lush, the jungle quiet and clean.

A gruesome anatomy lesson lay at my feet. Somebody yelled to get the radio. Somebody yelled for the ARVN interpreter, the one who grumbled about having to sleep on the ground. The army has cots and air mattresses for him, he kept reminding us. He would be leaving soon, he told us. Somebody yelled to check the wounded. All I could do was stare back and forth from the kids who didn't make a sound to the kids that would never make a sound. I'd seen horribly wounded Marines, but I'd never seen bodies laid open from head to feet, flesh blackened by the heat of exploding metal. I'd never seen tiny ripped organs and small splintered bones all mix-mashed together.

I'd been in country seven or eight months. I'd seen Marines blown to bits, cut in half. I'd seen traumatic amputations, legs shredded by land mines. I'd seen Marines drilled by AK-47 automatic fire. I'd seen glistening guts laying on top of guys who tried to hold themselves together. I'd never seen dead children.

That morning outside our gate Mama-san wanted choppers to take the wounded to the hospital in Chu Lai and the dead to the temple. They came the few kilometers to our position with a message from the NVA – proof that we couldn't protect them.

When I see the newspaper with the picture of the dead boy on the gurney I grab the kitchen counter to hold myself up. I fight to breathe. Blinding lights flash in my head. I know what is happening, but I can't get control.

I'd screamed myself awake from nightmares before, and I'd awakened sweaty with no recollection of a dream. I'd found myself lost in some sort of wakened dream state before. But this is overwhelming. I try to keep from being swept away in a tidal wave of heartbreak. I'm afraid I'm coming apart. I'm in hum like never before. I know what is happening, but I can't regain control, can't just move on.

Chapter 31
Power and Youth

The power I had as a 20-year-old is mind-boggling. I couldn't vote, but I could pick up the handset of PRC-25 field radio and call in a fire mission from the New Jersey. We didn't need officers or NCOs to handle getting support. They weren't even in the picture, unless they were monitoring the net. If we got into trouble, outgunned with nowhere to run, we got on the net and a shit storm rolled over the NVA.

Cobra gun ships fly 200 knots per hour, dive and climb. The eyepiece on the pilot's visor aims mini-guns at whatever he looks at. Artillery rains down in less than a minute. Jets shut down any movement toward us. Nobody has their head up shooting with air power pouring in on them. We sit back and smoke a cigarette.

If air power isn't available, because of bad weather or because they are stretched too thin with other missions, we are on our own. We ran for our lives twice. Shot off the beach.

The day is hot and lazy, the sun baking the white sand as we move in and out of a tree line that reminds me of a Ponderosa Pine desert in Eastern Washington State. Sometimes our six-man team walks through scrubby forest and low cactus that is transformed into tropical jungle with broad-leafed shrubs, banana trees and old gnarl Banyan trees. The terrain alternates between dense and not so dense. Sometimes we pass through a pod of deserted bunkers, low mounds of sand with timber-framed holes dropping four feet down into a narrow passageway that is lined with roughsurfaced, reddish-yellow kiln-fired masonry blocks from ancient Cham funeral towers. Down a gentle slope the forest thins into jungle and opens into a area rimmed by low cactus. We angle for the tree line on our right. On our left, the bare ground gently rises to meet jungle before dropping down to the beach. The sun is a white ball straight up, baking the white sand, reflecting the heat back up to our bare heads. We are moving like zombies when the oven erupts with automatic fire. Front and left flank.

We have to fight forward. We are outgunned, but made it a clump of trees. Nobody hit. Everybody spreads out and starts shooting two ways, front and left. If they push us toward the open beach we are fucked.

"Charlie, Lima Niner, this is 1-1-6; request gun ships at grid Sierra Tango 425333, over."

"1-1-6, this is Charlie Lima Niner; sid rep, over."

"Request immediate tac air, out."

Before I drop the handset I empty a magazine and hear the net crackle:

"Bad News, this is Jake. I copy your last. Fast movers coming ricky tic. I'll call for smoke as I approach your coordinates, out."

"Roger that. Purple haze will mark our pos, out."

I scream at Arnold to get ready to pop a purple smoke grenade when he heard Jake's O-3 Cessna but he was already rotating his shoulders, arm back to go long.

"Bad news, this is Jake. You have purple smoke, out."

Arnold has the handset and I hear him, "Roger that," and we grin at each other. I can see three NVA running in a crouch to our left. We just keep firing into the tree line front and left. I glance at Muledick: He fires a round from his grenade launcher, then picks up his 16 and empties a magazine, over and over. He's a strong, stocky, smilin' West Virginia tow-headed good ol' boy who never, ever seemed anything but happy-go-lucky. He got shot up in a fire fight later on.

The purple smoke Arnold threw is billowing in front of us. We were about to make a run for it when Jake flies a half circle over us, tips straight down and fires a willy peter (phosphorous target marker) round into the tree line across the clearing, about 60 meters from us. My guys are spread out and I yell as loud as I can, "We have fast movers danger close."

Seconds later an F-4 Phantom screams in at treetop level and drops a long silver cylinder that skitters along the ground and lays down a wall of orange fire. We duck as a whoom and blast of hot oily air rolls over us. Arnold and I stand up, watch a second jet come out of the pure blue at a 45 degree angle, disappear, then scream flat across our field of vision and let another long silver cylinder wobble down to the ground and hit with a tremendous bahwrack. We kiss sand.

All the colors are vivid – the gray jets against the green foliage, the silver bomb cylinders tumbling to the white sand. The orange napalm erupting, streaking through the jungle.

Barr, Muledick, and Stan come running over all bug-eyed and grinning.

"That was fucking awesome. I could see the fucking pilot; I swear he looked right at me," Barr said.

Some fly by.

"I cannot hear fucking shit! " Muledick laughs.

"Man!" Arnold shakes his head. "They were fucking on the deck, man. Jus' smokin', right fucking on top of us, man."

The tree line is still smoldering.

The first time we patrol north of Ky Phu ville we had a team of Cobra gun ships zoomin' out of the sky at 200 knots per hour and firing mini guns and rockets along side us and up ahead. They look so bad. They are shaped like a bad-ass dragonfly, sloped noses, narrow and tapered down to the tail. They are so streamlined the co-pilot sits behind the pilot, slightly elevated to see over his head.

They could dive and climb more like a jet than a chopper. They look awesome, sound awesome with mini-guns roaring. The rockets whoosh, then boom. The mini guns make a roar. And the chopper's jet turbines are howling.

I can't imagine what the NVA or VC felt with Huey gun ships zooming at tree top, door-gunners going deaf on M-60 machine guns humming long-linked belts of 7.62 mm rounds in sweeping arcs.

Huey's hover and swing in a circle firing rockets, slinging M-60 rounds from a pivot mount. Jets, cobras, gunships zoom down and in, roaring and blasting. Slow flying C-130 planes with multiple 20 mm cannons rigged in a Gatling system designed at Boeing firing so fast it sounded like a high-pitched buzz.

The shit is like a rock concert for us on the ground. At night the tracers are trippy. Puff the C-130, fires so fast the tracers formed solid red lines sweeping up and down, back and forth. A bad-ass light show. They could save your ass and blow your mind in one workout. Huey Choppers with mini guns and rocket pods work out right above grunts. Jets flash by trimming hedges in the foreground. They scream, roar and whine just above tree tops.

Then 500- and 750-pound bombs go bahrooom, bahroom as the jets bank and spiral up into the sky. It's weird seeing jets so close to the ground. Napalm cylinders skitter along the ground trailing a low wall of fire that roils up like an elongated, orange, A-bomb mushroom cloud. The rush from a danger-close air strike makes you giddy. Sleek jets screaming down to the deck.

I've watched a trail for what seemed like hours, then moved on top of a bunker and looked down a slope in the jungle just as NVA moved into an opening the size of a broom closet. There he is, visible from shoulders up and no idea he's been spotted. Hold your breath for a dead-on profile head shot.

I came around a bend in broad daylight and met a VC. We had the same reaction, freeze and go bug-eyed—that split-second look into startled eyes before your burst slams him on his back.

The first few times, I'm mesmerized by up-close sightings. And there they are, right in your field of fire, right in your sight picture. Early on I feel an instant of grab-in-your-gut before you squeeze the trigger. Later on, I feel a tingle of rush and then a calm. The world narrows and time slows down, almost stops. A target of smooth, light-brown face with dark eyebrows just below the brim of a black and green camouflaged bush hat. Slammed to the ground.

Sometimes it's the opposite – instantaneous reaction to stimuli – a clink, a wheeze. I snap out 18 rounds before I know it. When the tables are turned, new instincts send me assaulting the racket. Full auto. Guys that survive this kind of weirdness change. Rush in and see dark green uniforms maneuver, move up, try to surround us. It's cowboys and Indians freaked to the max, and lost boys dig it. Small ops mean up close contact, personal killing. Small teams have the element of surprise, and we got good at the game. We got addicted to it.

We handled our own casualties and sometimes theirs. The war becomes meaningless and boils down to survival. Casualties are briefly distracting, like a smudge on the windshield. Till I lose sight of something—how I used to be. Now, I just tell myself, "It don't mean nothing. Drive on." A killing machine can't be trained, just equipped. The real training is all on the job. With enough exposure, a green kid evolves, gets seasoned, gets potent. This is a process. It happens, and one day I feel it, and it feels right. We addicts know one world now. We forget home. We *are* home.

Chapter 32
Losing the American Dream

If our luck lasts, bush rats get snatched out of the bush, choppered to an airstrip and flown back to the real world. But tolls are on the books. The dues I pay learning survival mechanisms in combat erode all the connections to my emotional being, to my values and beliefs. It keeps me apart from the society I grew up with. I'm an alien. I feel like a zombie caught in a strange impasse. Same body, same neighborhood.

But nothing feels the same. My brain circuitry is out of phase with normal feelings and beliefs. My world has turned into a dangerous place. Everybody else's is benign and hunky-dory. Enjoy life. It's a given that life in America is sweet. But not for those who get lost in the dark night, who see too much and do too much. Back in the real world, familiar places aren't comfortable. Nothing seems relevant. Everybody around me seems clueless. Actually, I'm clueless about going back to civilization.

When I leave the military, no one says a word about what to expect, about how seeing too much violence, doing too much violence affects you. How my survival skills are all wrong for fitting back into society.

Or maybe it's that I know I'm close to the edge, an even darker edge, the edge of staying what I have become, and it scares me.

I knew about the protest movement, knew what to expect, knew they were right.

Perhaps during my time in Viet Nam, I promised

myself I wouldn't take the war "home." If so, that's the remains of my sanity, trying to bury it. The civil war in that little country had become a civil war in America, but I refused "to carry on here."

I want no part of any potential confrontation, and it is all about confrontation. A cop with a club or a can of tear gas is a menace and a menace pulls my trigger. I'm nervous, spooked about ending up in prison. I'm back in the world, but my mind clings to that zeroed-out meaning for life. Keep from getting killed. Keep my team on track to make it.

The dues I pay to enter the dark night become a haunting debt. A debt I can't get a handle on. I don't backtrack from the abyss, from the edge between life and death. There is no transition. No guide. I pretty much stay in a self-imposed exile. Alone.

Combat changes us so much that it is almost impossible to get back to what we were. We crossed a threshold and we can't come back. There is no one around me with this experience; no squad, no team, no fellow refugees. We come home alone, not as a unit, and there is no welcome, and there is no way I want anyone to know where I'd been. I bury it. I felt Simon and Garfunkle kind of hit it: "I am a rock/ I am an island." Stone cold and no way to thaw. An island that's only inhabited by certain types. An FNG again.

There is no one to tell me I'm not who I was and can't be who I am.

Family and friends want to erase it. I have to hide from it. Have to shitcan the life I'd been living and the death I'd been outrunning. So I keep running. I run from the demons. Denial is a life saver. I hide like the guerrilla I'd been and will always be.

You can't just walk away from a gunfight like it's nothing. So I put on new camouflage; bury my adventure. I try to walk the old walk, talk the old talk, get back with the American Dream. It isn't going to happen. That dream is shattered.

I go to my family doctor, a neighbor for whom I had done babysitting and yard work. I want to get a physical, make sure there were no defects from amoebic dysentery and one dose of clap. He's Dutch. He'd almost been drafted into the German Army at the start of World War II, but managed to work in a psychiatric hospital instead.

I wait in the examination room for the nurse to take my temp and blood pressure and stuff. She's about 30, slim with dark wavy hair. When I start to take my shirt off, she bolts. I scared her. This is how it is. I'd cross a street or walk down a hallway and people steer clear. I give off this essence of danger or something.

Dr. Klein comes in a few minutes later. He suggests I see a colleague of his.

"It's common to have some neurosis from combat," he said through a not-so-thick accent.

His shrink friend is Dutch also. I park my car blocks from the office, a different area each time. I slip quickly into the office, an apartment previously. I pay for it out of my pocket so there will be no record.

The office is dim. There's a window on Sixth Avenue near Wrights Park in Tacoma, Washington but the blinds are closed. I don't remember any book shelves, just a small desk in a corner. We sit across from each other in two chairs placed in front of the desk. He lights up a Camel; I smoke a Lucky Strike. There are long periods of silence.

"So, how is it going"?

"Well, I can't get going."

"Do you have any friends?"

"My buddy from the war is here."

"Do you see him often."

"No."

We sit quietly and smoke, and I come back about three more times. Finally, he makes an observation.

"In the war you had a lot of responsibility. Surviving. Keeping the men around you alive. Now, things don't seem as important."

I found out many years later that the psychiatrist went back to Holland and committed suicide.

Twenty-four years later I have to see a psychologist because my wife wants a divorce and we have a six-year old. The shrink asks about Viet Nam. I knew he hadn't been there, so I don't say much: I was a rifleman in an infantry company, that we humped to Khe Sanh for the big siege, lots of incoming. Then I got transferred to small teams. There was a lot more up close fighting then. That was it in a nutshell.

He asks, "Did you volunteer for small teams."

I said "No."

He says you have to volunteer for small team stuff. No, I say. I'd been shitcanned from the battalion for fighting another Marine on the Khe Sanh airstrip.

He gives me Rorschach Tests. I thought they were supposed to be obsolete. It's 1993. He has me interpret pictures. I remember one shows a woman lying in bed under a sheet with a man sitting on the edge of the bed looking distraught. She looks worried. It looks like around the time of 1850's or so.

I said, " She was sick, and he wants to help her, but they both knew it's hopeless."

His report says I'm the coldest vet he'd ever heard talk about Viet Nam, that I'm wound so tight I will snap, that I'm the ultimate loner.

There were other aliens like me everywhere, exiles in disguise, but it takes me 14 years after I come home before I find one. I meet a former Navy Seal on a construction job who'd been in country in 1968. We get tight. We talk a few times, and it's amazing to find someone who knows what I know. Then we parted.

It takes 16 more years before I go where I might find others who know. Early fifties, that's the age when Viet Nam combat vets start coming out of the hills, or we walk away from careers, families and drift in to the once-dreaded VA, unable to cope. The cumulative weight of guilt, denial and avoidance weakens psyches like drill worms in wood.

When I first come back two things become central to my day-to-day unsettledness – drugs ("self medication") and something to assuage the need for excitement and violence. A fix. Who knew back then what prolonged periods of high level adrenalin could do to someone's natural chemistry? Who knew about the long-term affect of sky-rocketed arousal? Of rejection by peers?

It's 1977. I'm a first-year apprentice electrician. I work with a fourth-year apprentice who is a Navy vet. He buys a new Porsche 924. I come to work one morning at the Trident Submarine Base and learn that police estimate he left a windy, 40 mph-posted rural road at about 100 mph in third gear. It's just days before Christmas. He'd brought a case of Wild Turkey in for gifts for the whole crew. He told me his girl friend said they were through. His blood alcohol tested negative. I knew what had happened. He said fuck it.

Does it feel good coming home from war? Not when I know I'll have to train troops. Send them to fight for a lost cause, to die and get maimed for nothing. I wish I hadn't come back. Even so, I figure I won't last long anyway. For years I was sure I'd answer the door to greet a shotgun blast. I don't know why exactly. Maybe an early grave still seemed in the cards. The world's a dangerous place, right? But the way we handle violence won't cut it back here, back in the world.

Some junkies survive, some don't. Who knew the addiction to adrenalin could affect one's judgment and subsequently the people around you. I know I am missing something. Walking high steel on construction jobs stoned feels good. I feel no urge to care about anybody when the life and death struggle isn't part of the connection. With my emotional self zeroed out, I'm no longer equipped to give and accept love, to become emotionally intimate. I can't step back and tell myself, "Look, this isn't Viet Nam. Make yourself over."

Guilt and denial become the connection with my emotional self. Bury it. My specialized knowledge fosters contempt, and I carry a chip on my shoulder equivalent to the 60-pound pack I humped up and down mountains in killing heat and steep terrain until death seems welcome.

The strangeness of being back in the real world, the hopelessness and alienation, combined with a sense of betrayal by national leaders, keeps mounting up.

For thirteen months I knew the war was wrong, a total waste. For nine months I dwelled in the underworld of humankind. The values I grew up with seem to be a sham. Nothing matters. The old American dream is snuffed in the dark night, crushed like a coconut under a tank tread.

Find that adrenalin fix and live for today. Forget about tomorrow. That is the way to deal with combat. And then the unexpected – I'm back.

Chapter 33
Night Shift

A flick of the neck flips the hood down, shields me from everything in a private dark world. All the stimuli around me are shut out. I have no sense of the environment around me. Everything but the bead of molten metal is shut out, surrounded in darkness. Maybe I'm an artist, maybe I'm fast and nasty. Welding on big contruction projects allows me to work alone. The welding hood shut helps isolate me.

Running a good bead sounds like bacon sizzling, looks like perfect, uniform ripples left by waves on a sandy beach.

Welding is best for loners on the beams of a unfinished roof along the Bay of San Francisco. Night shift and a warm breeze mixed with twinkling lights across the black water.

Inside dreamy darkness I jam my eyes over a molten puddle flowing evenly up a gap between two pieces of metal. The barely visible ring of red heat steers the puddle like something from a science video, a boiling sun spot or lava sealing a canyon.

Welders swagger, wear cowboy boots. For aluminum welding we use a Cobra Automatic Wire Feed Stinger. I have fresh air pumped inside my private world. Every condition must be perfect – heat, speed, wire position, argon gas shield – or a perfect bead could turn into a ball of grapes. In my sleep I dream of pass after pass.

At work I lay in thin layer after thin layer, with an inspector on my neck. It takes a week to complete a weld before it's X-rayed and etched with acid. When he comes around, I flinch my chin downward, strike an arc and flash him away.

Night shift is best. There is less supervision. It's quiet. A big construction site is spread out and the darkness and shadows are comforting. Welders work alone.

Chapter 34
Waiting to Come Home

Dear Mom and Dad,

The weather is hot. Hot, like wearing an electric blanket in a sauna. I haven't been assigned to a rifle company yet. I wish I could just stay at this base camp. I'm hoping they need a typist. I tell them I can type twenty words a minute, no mistakes.

"Dear Johnny,"

We watch the newsman standing in tall grass, hair flying and clothes flapping from a helicopter in the background. They report casualties, numbers per week or per battle. Ronnie knows you're there, knows there's a war going on. Yesterday he was standing on an apple crate in front of the TV, railing against the war, a seven-year old protester. He's fussy. He won't eat much, and says his stomach hurts. Dr. Klein says he's got the symptoms of an ulcer. I tell him you have to wait for your turn to come home. Haven't heard from you in quite awhile. Please write whenever you can.

"Dear Johnny,"

What's going on? The telegram says: "wounded in action... will return to duty." What happened, why didn't you tell us? Are you okay? Everyone is praying. It's been months since we got a letter. Please write whenever you can.

At first mail was an important connection to our old world. Later, we share any word from home. We really don't have private lives.

"Hey man, you got a letter. Who the fuck do you have back in the world? You *know* Jody's fuckin' your girl.

At least I don't have to worry; Jody nailed my girl way, way back, back when I was still a Fuckin New Guy.

Hey Stamps, when's the last time you got a letter from Rosie? Don't worry man. She's probably busy, so busy doin' your cousin she doesn't have time to write. Shit, cousin Jody."

"Ah know my Rosie is writin' me every day. Ah know it. It's jes' we never get no choppers out here an' when we fin'ly do, they don't bring jack."

"That bird gave us sustenance, man. One case of 5.56, one case of 7.76, one case of those new baseball grenades, and one letter. One letter to fuck with your mind, eh, Barr?

"Man, this is some shit."

"What, she say Jody got a bigger dick than you?"

"I'm fucked man, this is some serious shit."

"Man, serious shit would be dinner at my aunt's, man. She has to buy the pork chops at a special butcher shop, and the asparagus at the Pike Place Market. My mom makes the pie though."

"That ain't shit. My grandmother's Russian man. Nobody cooks like a Russian Jew grandmother."

"She knows we're keeping the fuckin' Russians from taking over your damn block, man. So what's the major malfunction? Jody scores again huh?"

"Fuck man, I told my sister there's good weed here and we got nobody in charge so we can trip in the jungle and she told her husband an' he fuckin' told some relative that works on some fuckin' congressman's staff that we're out here unsupervised and gettin' high."

"Well, no shit. She tell him the fuckin' gooks are stoned crazy too?"

"Unsupervised, my ass. Fuck, man, does she know the reason we're alive today is cause we don't have some pogue-ass lifer trying to run this team? Fuck congress. Man, those fuckin' know-nothing, never-been-anywhere fuckers back in the world get high too. Hell yes! What I want to know is if this dude your sister married has so much suck, can he get me a good deal on a '67, 340 cubic inch Dart Swinger so I can drive to New York City for some of that borscht or whatever it is you're so proud of?"

"As if you gonna make it out of here. How long you been in the bush, man... 11, 12 months? Man, you know there's a round with your name on it. Your time's about up, man. What you want a fuckin' Dodge for anyway? Fuckin' Mercury comes out with the Cougar and the first model wins *Motor Trend* magazine Car of the Year."

"Man, all I know is that I will never walk anywhere again and I will never starve again."

"Hey, if y'all rotate y'all come to my house and I'll cook a southern fried chicken dinner. No shit. With fried okra and grits and corn bread. Man, you ain't never had that shit, you ain't lived. Anyway; you may as well be fuckin' dade."

"Rotate my ass. The only way you gonna rotate, is when Charles hits you in a crossfire and spins you like a top."

"Man, that's cold. I'm here for the fuckin' duration, man."

"Well, since none of us is probably going to get out

of this motherfucker upright, anyway, let's hump down to Ky Phu Ville in the morning and drop a grenade in the river and let mamma-san make us a feast."

"That's eight, nine klicks man. You want to hump eight klicks, for fish heads and rice and that nasty-ass nuc maum shit?"

"Shit, if I knew we could get some weed down there, I'd carry your ass the whole damn way. We got to get one of us to the rear someday so we can get some smoke."

"Muledick's still got some butane, man."

"Fuck that shit. That shit nearly stopped my breathin'."

"There it is. That shit's dangerous."

"What we better do, is get ready to go out tonight and get some. It's been two days since we fucked with Charles, an' they might get bored and come stormin' right through our little home."

"Man, tha's your problem, man. You been here so fuckin' long, you are home."

Chapter 35
Landing at Travis Air Force Base

The flight back to the world is not good for me. I feel tense and uptight about how I'll have to spend the remainder of my enlistment contract. Five months and 20 days. I do not want to train troops. I know nobody should be going over there. I don't remember the stewardesses. Now I wonder what they thought about flying with a plane load of Viet Nam soldiers knowing the kind of reception we'd get for being part of a war that was so unpopular.

The day is bright as we walk across the tarmac and into a shed with long tables where military clerks check carry-on luggage. I set my small gym bag on the table. I worry for a moment about the .38 cal handgun. I worry about the ball of opium hidden in a roll of socks. I'd managed to get paperwork on the handgun. A thick set of orders included it as part of my personal gear. The clerk looks at the orders and never checks anything else. I have my handgun and dope.

We file into buses for the ride to Treasure Island Naval Base transition barracks. The Chinese guy I sit with is friendly and talkative. He'd been a payroll clerk in Guam. I tell him where I'd been and about my fear of having to train troops to go to Nam. He knew combat troops were eligible for early release from active duty. I'm eligible to get out. He takes me under his wing when we submit our orders.

"This guy is eligible for an early out. I've been a clerk and I know how things work, so make sure his orders go in the right pile."

The clerk looks at me and I can tell he can tell it would not be good to fuck with my desire to get out.

My new friend Bing's brother is an assistant professor at UC Berkeley. I may be able to get off base with him to visit his brother. But first he has to find a way to get off base, a privilege we enlisted men are not allowed. Bing has his shit together, though. He knows how to act around rear echelon dudes and what to expect. We go to the PX.

"Officers can come and go at this base," he said. "I'm going to buy some captain's bars, so don't act like anything is out of the ordinary. I'm supposed to provide proof of rank when you buy insignia."

He goes up to the counter cool as could be and puts the set of joined silver bars on the counter. He never bats an eye and the clerk doesn't ask for proof of rank, just rings it up. Impersonating an officer is some serious shit, but Bing pins the bars on his shirt and we walk off base.

His brother and some other grad students rent an old house just off campus. It's dim inside and has nice comfortable furniture. It looks like a house a widow would live in. Everything quaint and old and in its proper place.

My new friend and I walk onto campus. We walk by a group of hippies who are harassing a Navy ROTC kid. The kid is trying to explain that he doesn't support the war. He has his uniform shirt off hanging around his waist. The crowd is taunting him. It's Spring 1969 and the protest movement is going strong. I can't tell if the guy is intimidated or just doesn't buy into the military trip. Lots of guys go through ROTC to buy time.

We walk to a grassy area on campus. I see a girl lying on her stomach studying. I'd been in a setting like this many times at the University of Washington.

"I'm going to meet her," I say.

"Yeah, right. Like she'll have anything to do with you."

I remember that she is slim, wearing shorts and has dark hair.

"Hi. Are you studying for a test ."

"No. Just doing some reading."

I probably asked her what her major was. I probably said I'd been a student at the University of Washington.

"Are you going to school here now?" she asks.

I should have lied, but how long could I carry that off?

"No. I just got back from Viet Nam."

I remember the banter came to a sudden halt. She didn't insult me. There was just this impasse. End of conversation.

"Well, did you get her name and number?"

"No. I couldn't think of anything to say to her. We didn't even talk really."

Bing offers to take me with him on a weekend to Lake Tahoe with his brother. I decline.

"It will be fun, there'll be women, you know, for hire."

It sounds right, but it doesn't feel right. Maybe it is the idea of celebrating. It puzzles me that I don't want to go. It will take me a long time before fun will be a concept I can grasp.

Back in the barracks I'm assigned to, I see three Marines surrounding a small Mexican Marine, harassing him about something. In a second I'm pissed off. I get in the middle of it and the three melt away. The Mexican is a sergeant from Moses Lake, Washington. I'd lived in Moses Lake for a year when I was about four.

"I've got an uncle who lives in South San Francisco," I tell him. "I can't stand it here. I called him. He's going to come get me tonight. Why don't you go to his house with me?"

At dinner my uncle John asks the two of us what we are going to do now that we're getting out of the service. The other Marine's reply strikes me as odd. He says he's going to go back to Moses Lake and take care of his younger sister, make sure she gets through high school. I have no thoughts about my family.

This is definitely a huge change for me, and I'm not used it at all. On the base, MPs follow me whenever I leave the barracks. I go to the PX to look at albums, and the MPs stand at the end of the aisle watching me. The whole rear echelon military atmosphere makes me uptight.

My cousin and her boyfriend set me up for a double date. The girl had been Miss South San Francisco or a contestant in some pageant. She's fun-loving, not a stuck up beauty queen at all.

We ride in the back seat going somewhere. My cousin sits right next to her boyfriend in the front. I keep my distance from my date. I feel inhibited, strange.

"Did you ever smoke dope over there?" she asks.

"Yeah, a little bit."

She leans toward her friends in the front seat.

"Wow, he got high in a war."

My cousin's boyfriend glances back at us from time to time. I can tell he's trying to get me to loosen up a bit. Finally, he takes a high speed left turn that slides my date right into my lap. I know she's a little intrigued and willing to have a good time, but I'm uncomfortable. About what I don't know, but I just can't make a move.

At the base I ran into Guy Yancy, my friend from boot camp. He had gotten wounded and spent most of his tour in Hawaii. He is shocked at the way I look. He convinces me to go home with him to Astoria, Oregon, before returning to my family. He tries to help bring me back into the world.

We hang together in Astoria for about 10 days in the Spring of 1969, and then I go to my parents' home, to a place of edgy impasse.

They want to help. They think I should write about it, build a scrap book from pictures I sent home.

Cameras are for lying. I can't write. I can't concentrate long enough to read a paragraph in the newspaper. Out of the blue, I tell my mother I don't want to meet any girl that wants to get married. I already know I can't connect with my old world.

Something won't let me relax, won't let me sleep. I can't figure it out then, but now I know I had some guilt, some shame. I can't just drop back into society and pick up where I'd left off. I knew I'd had plans for the future at one time, but they seem to be a mockery. Spending 10 days with someone who has been there doesn't bring you back. I calm down a little, but I can't come home. I've seen too much. I know too much.

At Treasure Island Naval base I exuded the essence of a killer. I'd been out of the bush a week. It peered out of my eyes. It showed on my clenched jaw. I was not afraid of anything but myself. I was steeped in violence, and I'd been around so much death.

I wanted to meet women and be with regular people, people of my old world, but I have nothing in common with them or their dreams. I couldn't close the door on the world I left. It was too real and too recent. I could not pretend I hadn't seen what men will do to each other.

Everyone my age condemns the war. I understand this. Better than anybody. Not just the ugliness and grief. Not just the hopelessness. I know all about the repugnancy, but I'd been addicted to the fascination of it. And now I'm out of it, and nothing feels right. We can't just survive it and then forget it.

I'm ready to go back. I feel guilty for making it. Why me? Is there something I'm supposed to do now? There is something I'm good at, something I understand and I can get paid for.

I sign up to be a mercenary for the Lon Nol government in Cambodia in 1970. I'll stop floundering in my old world, go back to what I know, to my expertise. I'm supposed to meet him in Sydney, Australia, but decide against it at the last minute. I wouldn't have my old team.

When I first came home, I wished I hadn't. None of the goals that had seemed important mean anything. I have no desire to go back to school except to collect the paltry GI bill allotment of $130 dollars a month. I only want the GI Bill to get back at my government. The military hasn't prepared me for any job but killing. That's something I really became good at, and there's no use for it.

A few weeks after I had been home, I get on a plane to Brooklyn to see Barr. He'd gotten out a couple weeks after me. I send him a telegram and tell him my flight number. I have to see someone like me. His brother-in-law owns a furniture store. He asks us if we'd spend nights in the store with rifles and blow away anyone who breaks in. While I'm there I stop at the New York office of Aramco Oil.

"I'd like to apply to be a pipe line guard in Saudi Arabia," I tell the receptionist.

She looks really puzzled. "We don't have jobs like that."

I feel a lack of responsibility, lack of connection. But the fear of what I can do shakes me to the core. I'm scared. Sitting in my parents' house I know I could line my family up and kill them if it came down to surviving another day. In Viet Nam, surviving was the essence of existence. I'm dead inside, no emotions. I'm aware I went through some sort of breakdown in Viet Nam.

I accepted what men were capable of doing to each other untill it no longer mattered. I accepted that young men were killed and maimed for nothing.

There is no honor and glory in serving your country, in using violence against a race who has a different form of government than ours. I accept that women and children are killed because they are in the wrong place or that we are in the wrong place. Killing has become part of me; it was as mechanical as brushing my teeth.

I'm afraid of what I am, what I can do. So I don't really come home. I stay hidden in the tangles of guilt and a special knowing. I feel lost. I can't stay in the jungle. I can't find the world I left.

Chapter 36
Shattered Dream

"When asked about my dreams of the future, I simply cannot comment on them. I can't even imagine the future."

– Joe Fiala, Marine Corps Viet Nam Veteran

In combat I shut down all feelings. I've seen enough blood, taken enough lives. I became disconnected from a civil world. The arm of my emotional radar stopped sweeping. I die inside and this enables me to keep going, to accept death and to forget it. My spirit dies and I figure it's just a matter of time before I'm gone.

Being in a rogue team out on our own without supervision may have been a two-edged sword. We didn't have a fuck-up who could get us killed, but we didn't have anyone to gauge when we had gone too far.

In his book *Shattered Dream: America's Search for its Soul*, Walter T. Davis writes: "In a war of attrition (body counts) soldiers gradually lose their moral bearings. Their narratives about the war depict a gradual deterioration of order, disintegration of moral character, alienation from military establishment and those at home."

I have already said that I changed. I was 20 years old and had spent 13 months in combat. When I got home I felt 20 years older and I knew I was emotionally dead.
Early in my tour I promised myself that if I made it I would go to the *Seattle Times* and tell the true story. What a waste the war was. What we were doing to their country and their people. How nothing the Americans could do

would change the outcome. How we couldn't hold that country together.

All of us Americans had been duped. But when I came home I didn't want to tell anyone what I knew and nobody wanted to hear it. So maybe I was still working for our government. Our leadership swept it under the carpet and I stuffed it, kept it buried for 30 years. Silence is a collaborator. I felt guilt and shame for having been part of it. I felt fear that the violence I was capable of could ignite in a flash.

I had to keep my nightmare private. I became a loner, though I could put on an act to appear normal. I could become someone else on the outside, but inside, my heart blackened.

Perhaps nothing seemed right or felt right about my old world because my identity had been destroyed. I changed from the scared and appalled kid to a killer.

Chapter 37
Trying to Reconnect

I'm an alien. I don't belong here. I go to a bar and spin around at the open doorway. Young people are laughing and carrying on. Too silly, too weird, too clueless.

I wish I hadn't come back. I didn't want anybody to know what I was thinking, where I'd been. I feel haunted, out of touch with this world. A friend I'd met in training is home from the war. He'd gotten an apartment in the University District and starts back to school a couple months after getting home. I wonder how he picked up where he'd left off.

Nancy had written me from Western University north of Seattle.

"Come up and I'll get your head straight," she wrote.

Okay, this will be good. We knew each other in high school; we'd fooled around a little the summer we graduated. She is cute, athletic. I race up there eager to connect with someone from my old world. She and her sister and sister's boyfriend are sharing a house. A good sign. I feel so ready to be with a woman who knows me, knew the innocent boy I was. Maybe I can connect with my old world. I need everything she has to offer.

She's caught up in the protest movement. Right away she asks, "Why hadn't you come to Hawaii before you'd gone to boot camp? Why didn't you go to Canada?"

Everything gets awkward and when it's time to crash, she looks me in the eye and says,

"I won't sleep with a baby killer."

I leave and drive across the state to visit my brother and sisters at Washington State University.

I get pulled over for driving too slow.

I want something but I don't know what or where it is. I should have gotten discharged over there, in a world that I understand.

The only thing I can feel is hate. Fuck the USA! I remember the fantasy I concoct while collecting parts of Marines in a poncho for a dust off (medevac chopper). I visit the Pentagon. I breeze right by those poster-boy, dress-blues, embassy-duty Marines with an M-16 under my coat. I bust that Joint Chiefs of Staff meeting up and go down killing.

I carry the shame of serving and the guilt of surviving. A round through the heart with my jinxed .38 cal sidearm I'd brought home and I can be free. A death is a death. I'll do it. As distant as I have become from my family, and from everyone else, my family is what saves me. I think, "I can't shame them." I'm already dead, but they're still alive. I can't hurt anyone anymore."

This doesn't solve my dilemma. Two days later I'm ready again to put a round through my heart.

I fight off the impulse twice.

I try to take this shattered dream and get it together. Get the girl, get married, get the job. That plan seems so straightforward. There's nothing to it. Shoulder the disillusionment, the betrayal. Load the contempt like an extra three hundred rounds of gun ammo and keep humping. It ain't steep, it ain't hot, and it ain't dangerous. You can quit anytime, say fuck it. Just stay away from weapons.

Twenty years later and I'm still struggling to pick

up the dream. It's crumbling. I'd been pushed out of a job. My wife is home with our new baby and frightened. I feel an opportunity, a chance to give her financial security. I'm way, way up, installing a warning beacon on the tip top of a crane at the docks in Seattle. It's a bright, sunny day with an asphalt dock like a dark pool, seven stories below. No safety belt, no shame. Just a quick surge, and it will be over. I nearly let go. Then I grab the lighting mast and hug it, trembling.

Chapter 38
Lost Boys

There are no gilt-edged dreams in the dark night. Back in the world, blank dreams run by undetected. Why did I wake up calm but sweaty? I knew I'd been dreaming, but of what? Sometimes I woke up in a frenzy, but I had no clue what it was about. Something deep in my subconscious shook me. Waking nightmares trashed me. Little bumps in the night triggered responses without waking me.

Triggers like music, scenery, the sound of Huey choppers chugging around Ft. Lewis and McChord Air Force Base launched me back to Viet Nam. A fancy hotel in Seattle with an intercom system in the headboard triggered a sid rep (situation report). The woman I'd spent the night with had to get up early for work. Five a.m. When she is about to leave, she rouses me.

"You were mumbling after the wake up call," she says. "What does, 'all secure negative contact' mean?"

Chapter 39
Falling for the Goddess

Fear gradually dissolves like fog burning away in rain-cooled heat, and your thinking changes. After a few firefights, you're always ready to go and reflexes take over when the shit hits. I'd dive into that cool, slowed-down, dig-it zone. You feel jazzed, not fearful.

See too much action and the violence will thrill you. The first burst you fire is all reflex and then you're moving and looking for targets. You love it when you spot them. Fear that used to seize your guts like a fist clutching clay burns out like an untended joint. You stay in the moment and it's all jazzed up. You're supercharged, guts resonating at M-16 muzzle velocity with no kick back.

Smooth and cool. Keep shooting, line up a couple grenades, straighten the pins. Move Cronin more right. Fire a burst. Tell Smitty to keep shooting. Rig up a big charge with a short fuse. Fire a burst. The air is electric; cymbals crashing, drum heads shredding. It's pure hard rock—Jimi, Mick, good god! Tina rolling sweat in a hiked up miniskirt.

Your guts are zinging and your mind is cool and it's focused – like sex on coke. Come baby, get there. Short bursts. Move. Move up. Get on the net. Short bursts. Short bursts. Oh yeah. Let's get it on. Get on the net. Get some big guns. Get some gunships, jets.

I remember the day, a hot and still day—blue sky, blue water, white sand. It was the day after we'd made contact again north of our position. A friendly ville was about eight klicks south of us and all the fight we wanted in front of us. Sitting at the edge of the surf on our beach, our

Shangri-la, I knew things were different. It was downtime in paradise. I was calm. I felt something strange, something that went entirely against the grain of civilization: Yeah *wegotcontactgridXrayDelta350667—rogergunshipsinboun dwillmark yankeesmoke.Out.*

Close calls supercharge the rush. I'm in your backyard and I'll jump in your shit. We will fuck you up. We want to play with your best. We want to buc buc with the NVA.

"You know Barr," I say, "I don't feel cold-blooded, but I love contact. I'm into this shit. It's weird. I love the people, you know, the villagers down in Ky Phu. But if we get this area pacified, I want to move on to another hot area."

"Yeah man, it's cool," he says. "You know, it's grooving on the excitement and the challenge."

I loathed the people that got us into this mess, hated the flag waving, "We just need more troops." Lifer desk jockeys. I'd taken the post-grad exam of combat and aced it.

I'd changed. It was gradual and seductive and it made me feel strange. At the same time I felt empowered with new insight, intellectual capability, whatever. I could solve any problem, figure out what was making a guy lose it, knew how to bring them around. I called it my "new understanding." Show me famous artwork by the masters, I could interpret it. Some high-level cognizance had popped into my head – I got it. I wasn't just some pawn in the military strata, I was king. I could get things, ammo from the army, help from the Vietnamese chain of command. I could fly with a spotter pilot and get the best bomb damage assessment of the day for all of I Corps. I could ride with the Navy Swift Boats and eat in the officers' mess.

But I didn't understand how the "groove" affected me. I didn't know it but I was changed for good. I could never be able to just walk away from something so strange. I wouldn't know that for 30 years. You feel like one of a kind, a freak. Nobody who hasn't been there can comprehend where you've been. You may bury it, but it's there. Psychic scar tissue. Psychic lesions embedded and getting inflamed, irritated. Black worms mining the folds of your brain. I shot past my youth, got jaded, old quick. I left my soul somewhere on that spit of land near 1-1-6.

The change is incremental. In combat you make it and shake it later. It's not about reflection, it's about shedding the slime stains on your psyche. Shucking the shock before it sends you catatonic. Hard trembling was my double-on-the-rocks, my toke, my six pack after a hard day. Muscles shudder wildly and I'm laughing, "Those mother fuckers tried to do me." That's it. Reflection can't happen.

Feelings for wasted or maimed buddies are snuffed. Steel myself or lose it. Acceptance and denial pull my emotional connections. Only instincts and savvy count. Later, avoidance becomes my way of coping. Just keep moving on. In the fleeting moment I see myself as I roll over a dead soldier, I have to blow that image.

Best friends die. "Better him than me." Stay cool. Slap some C-4 on that friendship and blow it. Take any handy items, poncho liner, boot laces, whatever, from his corpse and drive on. Killing changes me until death no longer phases me. Even the death of an enemy soldier, his uniform just a little different color than my jungle utilities, his young face, now blanked, shaped a little differently around the eyes, the skin a different hue. The letter in his pocket was on flimsy crisp paper, the family picture covered in cellophane could ripples my thoughts for a moment and then get smothered. But for the child in her arms, at her knee, this could be me. *Uh huh, fuck that shit. Drive on.*

My teammates get wasted, one in the flash of a rigged 105 mm round buried on a trail; some as I desperately tried to stop them from pumping out. Some I find when the smoke clears. Twice I carry what is left of a friend to the dust-off chopper. No grieving, no honoring, no promises to contact their family, if I make it. I knew them intimately – their families, their high school glories, their girlfriends or wives, their dreams. Now they fade like a jungle mountain at sundown.

We drop it all, our thoughts boiled down to the bone. Plan the next fight, get everything ready. Pull the stops. Check the map, plot an on-call artillery fire mission and give it a call sign. If we need it, it'll be there most ricky tic. Kick the hornets' nest. Make it then shake it. We get tight, look after each other, help each other find a rush, make another wake up. Lost boys. I'm Peter Pan run amuck.

When team continuity is unbroken by rotation dates, transfers, wounds, dysentery or language school, business thrives. Killing's our business and business is good. I get real aggressive. Especially, with 1-1-6 I got like this. High, high risk became part of my "new understanding."

This is living life to the hilt, meat on the line every day. I'm a twenty-year-old cruising in the dark night. This new reality fits fine. Crazy punt returners don't worry about getting hurt; they want the ball. Lost boys don't worry about getting hit; they crave action. Maybe the chances of surviving get better in a team like this. Maybe you just need some luck.

We'd found a hot area.

Our only aspirations were to stay busy and be left alone. There was no division of labor, just teamwork. We were tight. We didn't think of ourselves as Marines, just highly motivated thrill seekers and shepherds of the fishing ville south of us.

There could be no team like 1-1-6 anywhere, anytime in the real world. Never like a combat team that just emerges from misfits too bright, too savvy and too experienced to suffer authority when the stakes are high. Once we got civilians relocated from Phu Yen ville north of us to an abandoned portion of Ky Phu ville south of us, it was balls to-the-wall gang warfare with the NVA and their Viet Cong pals.

We fought for the thrill and to survive. Our mission statement would have been the basic slogan of the guys in the thick of it. "Get some." No marriage could match the closeness of partnerships formed from a shuffled deck of replacements and dealt to battalions, teams, outposts hidden in pockets of paddies, mountains and patches of jungle.

Teams mysteriously morphed during the individual 13-month tours of combat. I ended up in a microcosm that was a mix of brotherhood, survival and playing at the edge. It works or it's over. You get with the program. Guys arrive in country and fill a slot somewhere. They get wiped out, wasted, culled or tuned in. There's an intrinsic filtering system and there's some serendipity.

Somehow a core of a good team forms up and guys have to make the team. You didn't get assigned and that was that. We had tryouts and cuts. We picked our spot and we picked our name. We tried out gungy guys they sent out and we sent some back. Some got themselves out after a firefight or two, found ways back to the rear.

Chapter 40

Seeing Too Much

Asshole supervision is the hardest to endure. Humping through the Truong Suong Mountains to Khe Sanh a kid fell out with heat exhaustion. The Co Roc and Truong Son mountains surrounding the Khe Sanh Valley are brutal, steep and so dense you can't swing a machete. Canteens of water couldn't cool him down. He lay burning and quiet. A sergeant tries to kick the kid up as his red face started to pale. The corpsman works fast and smart, hooks up intravenous fluid. This guy knows his shit.

"Call in a medevac."

"No fucking way," the sergeant growls.

"Get a medevac, he's turning white; he's going into heatstroke."

"No medevac, get him on his fucking feet."

The life saver we carry in canteens is gone and so is the kid. A fellow grunt becomes a killing load on up the mountain. I hate this kid for dying. He is killing me. Trading off carrying the corpse we make it to the top. Tall grass is thick in the clearing. I drop him, move off by myself, flop onto my back. I'm ready for it to end. I'm not hiding, not digging in. Come, walk up on me. Fine. Kill me. The chopper comes to pick up the body.

Our squad has to stand another squad's position while they recon the area. I decide to write a letter. Looking around the foxhole, I find a tablet, a partially written letter by the sergeant who thinks he's an ass-kicker. He's boasting about keeping the column moving, how he'll probably get a field promotion. I spread the word. A day or two later, an opportunity is right for the code to kick in. We take a few sniper rounds. We get on line in the crisp brown grass.

"Move up," says the ass-kicker sergeant, getting on his feet.

Nobody moves, just open up with short bursts. He's hit from so many directions he spins like a top. Payback. He probably got his medal, though.

This team has got their shit together, all of us baptized, confirmed, ordained in the order of killing, in the church of Escaping Death Still. We handle everything fine; stay in control, find our fix, temper the madness.

There's no livestock shooter, no finger collectors, no sadists, no skaters. When you see someone like us in a rear area, we're easy to pick out. The look is haunted, deadly. We don't talk to anyone unless there's another bush rat around. We find each other. We don't go to the club, don't drink, don't watch a movie. We find a place to be alone or with each other to get high. We want to get back to the bush. We like the juice. We live for it. We help each other get there.

A couple of us had requests for R&R turned down for 11 or 12 months. We stopped thinking about R&R. Fuck it. Swim in the South China Sea. Share a joint. Hear a little rock and roll. That's a vacation in the bush, a rare escape to a dark bunker and laughter. A candle makes friendly shadows, softens zombie faces in a sweatless sheen.

Chapter 41
Letting Your Guard Down

There's a ville eight klicks away. Go there, see who you're protecting. Drink some tea; try their language. Give out medicine. Laugh with the kids. Watch something beautiful you'll never have. The kids chirp, "Co Tui, Co Tui a dai!" Tui glides by. An angel in black silk pajamas.

One day she ventured with her friends near our strip of the beach, far from their ville. We're lounging. They see us, giggle then bolt like frisky thoroughbreds on a crisp Montana morning. She is the fastest—tall and svelte with three feet of black shiny mane flowing behind her. I stare in awe at this flat-out grace framed by blue-green, white-crested sets rolling up to the pure white track she flies over. I am stunned by a glimpse of something missing from my life.

I can still see her. She's a super model without make up and attitude. She's Flo Jo without the ripped body. She's lithe and toned from life in a fishing ville. In the ville, sipping tea with her family, she is shy, composed. Her friends laugh, give me sidelong glances.

A dream runs through my head as I try hard to make my Vietnamese sound fluid. She would never want me. She does not see a ticket to the good life. She has no ken of that. For a second time, she sees a boy from a different world. She knows what I am. She knows what I do.

There's nothing waiting for a good warrior after a hard day. We can't go too long without getting some action.

We become savvy, brave, and desperate for contact. The pace slows. We ask for another assignment. We are ready to give up the only beauty in our life, our pos – wide river, exotic terrain, warm ocean and spectacular beach. Captain Champion's AO is hot, backup hot. We call him on the net. "Can you get us over there?" we ask. But our commanding officer won't release us.

Our team shrinks, then grows – new bone around the marrow. Gungy ones think they want some of this. Allen comes out, gets in one firefight and cut his own foot to get back to the rear. Hollywood Marines. Cronin and Kieg go where you tell them not to. Some walk, like Marcos, not run through clearings even after you warn them. Some have been skating, haven't been in the shit. They freeze. Eyes wide, faces paled in terror – wonderful targets. We pick up their remains.

We pick up guys who have been in country but not bloodied. Then we lose some who seemed untouchable. They've been there, seen it all, have their shit together. You don't grieve for the new guys, or anyone else, even the friends you're tight with.

We break off from a team and form a new one. We pay a small price for messing with the chain of command. Someone else gets the medals; I'm reduced in rank. Petty things. My pay drops eight bucks a month, $85 per month with combat pay. I never see it, it stays on the books. Nowhere to spend it in the bush. Kill for peace? Hardly. Kill for kicks. We knew our chances. CAP guys took 80 percent casualties. We deal with it. We cheapen our lives.

We're not really aware of it.

Chapter 42
Bobby and Cronin

I strain to heft Bobby onto the floor of the dust off as the door gunner spews his guts. Must be an FNG or a clerk going for a joy ride. Bobby Kieg is half gone, but I can hardly lift him off the ground. There is no mess. The flesh left on the upper-thigh stumps is cauterized by heat of a land mine blast.

It's hot, perfectly still when I come up on him lying face up in a small crater of sand on the brush side of the wide spot on the trail. He has nothing on but a shirt and cartridge belt. No expression on his face. Not a trace of blood, pants, boots, nothing. Gone from his balls down. I back up and wait a few minutes, listening for any eyes on me, then crawl in.

Had I missed it the day before or was it newly planted? I came through here the day before by myself. It looked bad when I'd reconned this area, especially along a string of deserted hooches and bunkers – too perfect for an ambush, too hidden.

This much I knew. The Vietnamese could not hold their country together and neither could we. It's all a huge waste. But then judging the world fades away. You're where the action is and now it feels good. Stinks too, really sucks.

Bobby was a strong, handsome, had-his-shit-together Midwestern kid, the kind you liked being around. Dead hours after giving him and Cronin the okay to head down to the ville.

"Just don't go down the interior; stay on the beach," I warn. I stay at our pos with the radio. I'm laying in my hammock hoping for sleep.

I crawl back up to Bobby. Laying my face against his ribs I probe my bayonet under his body feeling for booby traps. Slipping it in tenderly, feeling for anything solid, listening for a metal-on-metal scrape, hoping for smooth slices of uninterrupted sand. No bumps. Still unsure, I lie head-to-head, using him for a shield. I dig one hand into the sand, reached under his chin and tried to drag him to me. I can't budge him.

How much room do I have to hang in the very place that spooked me yesterday? I get on my knees and hug him to me, stand up and move to the other edge of a clearing. I take his .38 cal. and put the holster in my pocket. I find the letter to his wife – another decision to make later.

I call in a dust off, land it right there in the clearing, not knowing, but knowing the down draft won't set off another mine. Two down today. I'd already found Cronin face down on the beach with his foot blown off. A swift boat sent a skiff in and took him to Chu Lai.

As the bird settles in, I crouch over Bobby. Hug him up to me. Carry him to the chopper.

I'm beat down and so tired. I make my way to the ville, to the river. It's too hot, the radio too heavy to hump back up the beach. I hail a fisherman pushing his way up stream. When he ignores me I whistle a round right by him and call him over again.

The Butcher, one of our Vietnamese sidekicks, shows up and wants a ride back to our pos. I have no use for him, but say okay. The Butcher messes with prisoners who are tied up. Cuts them. You have to watch him. The fisherman stands at the back, single-oar pushing us quietly along. The Butcher stands up, then falls in. He thrashes wildly, grunting in terror.

I tell the fisherman to keep going, my 16 in my lap – okay by me if he drowns. The fisherman is trembling, freaking out. I say go back and pull the Butcher into the narrow skiff. I figure I own him now.

On the way up I call in a sit-rep about the casualties. Get back to our pos and go to my bunker, wondering about the letter. Should I have given it to the door gunner? His wife gets a telegram and days later, a letter? Hold it till later? How much later? I never did anything with it. I don't know what I did with it. I can't remember.

Bobby gets wasted and Cronin maimed on an easy day, a day off. We were the only ones at our pos that day. Arnold got pulled into the rear with no replacement. Barr was in Da Nang at language school, Doc in Bangkok. That means a day off.

I'm trying to sleep, lying in my hammock, trying hard. I'd told Bobby and Cronin what I'd found going the interior route the day before. I'd been trying to turn off my brain when the panicked ARVN flew into my bunker.

"All the Marines dead. All the Marines dead."

I grab the radio and map and hustle eight klicks down the beach. Find Cronin face down, motionless where the brush meets the beach. No bleeding but his foot looks like a bowl of spaghetti on the end of his ankle. I'd called the Swift Boat on the way down. Their skiff is buzzing in as I kneel and touch Cronin on the shoulder. He screams. The swifties have morphine and in a bit Cronin with his face still in the sand fills me in as best he can. After the blast killed Bobby, Cronin was disoriented, tried to make his way to the beach, stepped on a toe popper.

"Where did it happen? Was it after the hooches? Did you see any hooches on your right?"

"No."

I'd have to go in and find Bobby. I have to pick a route to go look for him up the beach and back down the interior, or go in here and backtrack him. I decide to go in here and work my way back toward our pos. The swifties are lifting Cronin onto a canvas stretcher.

"You're going home Kronnie. No sweat now, man. You can still be a cop. No problem."

The swifties find the .38 I'd loaned Cronin and toss it to me. The handgun with the jinx. I'd loaned it twice. Twice there'd been trouble.

Marcos, a replacement, was arrogant, off the block from Chi town. He didn't last long. I watched him diddy-bop through a clearing during a patrol. I gave him some strong conversation. This was basic shit. I was in the rear getting reprimanded for punching a Biet Lap who pointed his rifle at me when Marcos got head shot standing in a clearing. I didn't know him well. These were my last losses, my magic now tarnished. I thought I had everything cold. The charm. Bad News Point Man. Fuck it. We're going up north. Get some payback.

Maybe getting called into the rear to get my wrist slapped cost Marcos.

One night when there are too many stars out, we stay in. I let a Biet Lap stand guard on top of our bunker. No danger of attack under the bright night. I'm reading "One Flew Over The Cuckoo's Nest."

In my hammock, I feel a spray of water splash in

through the window hole cut into the bunker. I think I know what it is.

I go up on top of the bunker as the guy is tucking himself back into his pants. I ask him in Vietnamese why he's pissing into my bunker? He claims it's raining. I tell him I guess I'll have to tell his honcho this guy's too lazy to go off somewhere and piss. This shakes him up. Their honchos fuck with them pretty bad. He swings his rifle up at my chest. My fist just snakes out to his chin without thought, though I do pull the punch. Punching a Vietnamese is a no no. He flies off the bunker. I jump down as he gets to his feet, charges me and rams his head into the corner roof joist. Knocks himself out.

Our corpsman hears the commotion, starts to tend to the guy.

"Leave him. He's got his own corpsman."

Chapter 43
Overload

We capture 13 NVA soldiers, one an officer, north of our compound. Ooten kills another officer point blank with an M-79 round square in his face. The guy had hit Ooten with an AK-47 burst. He took rounds in the shoulder and jaw. The officer had been apart from the group when we rush them. Surprised them in broad daylight. Ooten is not feeling pain, he is ecstatic. He knows he's going home. Home to his wife who used to sit on the bench with him at high school football games, along with other couples who were married.

"Muledick, (his nickname), do you want this AK the guy tried to do you with?"

"No. Give it to Jake. I'm going home," he says with enthusiasm, spraying blood through broken teeth and smashed jaw bone.

He is one of the early 1-1-6ers. Jake is the spotter pilot I'd gone up with one time. We tie the prisoners' wrists behind their backs and lead them out to the beach for dust offs to the rear. We keep them standing in a group. A few Biet Laps (our Vietnamese sidekicks) come up the beach. They'd been monitoring the net (field radio network). Our policy is to leave them back when we went in for a fight. The Biet Laps start hassling the captured, being real bold. In an instant 16s roar full auto, mowing the prisoners down. Backs arch as rounds and guts flew out of their torsos. We are screaming at them. I grab an NVA and pull him away from the massacre. He's talking wildly. From behind, a Biet Lap shoots the back of his head off point blank. I let him down slowly, his brains spilling. My ear hammers in pain. I look quick for Barr and the others. Nobody down. Prisoners lay tangled like a clump of reddish-green driftwood. We stand stunned, rooted in the sand. Blank. Those rounds could have killed us. I radio HQ, change the sid rep from thirteen captures to thirteen kills. We dust them off, walk back to our pos.

Beyond the stain of murder, the beach is white and pristine, giving way to short cactus and low-growing bush brush on our left, blue-green sets rolling and frothing on our right. I can't remember the walk back, except for one thought. I envision myself going over, fighting for the NVA.

A chopper lands within minutes of our arrival. I'd only seen an officer in the bush twice in a year and here are two, a colonel and a major. One talks, the other writes. I calmly advise them how it went down. Stuck out here fighting, killing – yeah, that is us. Atrocity is not us. We don't shoot pigs, much less captured NVA.

The colonel says I'm under criminal investigation and they leave. I don't think they brought any supplies or mail. We group in my bunker and talk a little about our sidekicks. In the rear they are known as brave little freedom fighters. For us, the divide widens. For me, I still have my two fantasies – fighting for the NVA and slipping into a meeting of the Joint Chiefs of Staff with an M-16 to go down killing.

One day I succumb to agonizing despair. Walking and weeping, I feel like everybody has left and I'm alone with the cold sky, the murky river and deserted beach. Days before, headquarters had radioed for me to come in and sent out a chopper. I watched it come and go from a tree line outside our wire. I can't remember if it was about the order to see a shrink or the reprimand for punching the Biet Lap who pointed his rifle at me.

I've hit the bottom. I walk by our corpsman, tell him I'm going in and veer right out the wire. No rifle, no C's. Just impulse. I wear two grenades and a .38 handgun. One second I'm walking toward my bunker, and the next I'm headed down the beach.

Gray sky blows down on my neck. The ocean backs up, churning like a giant washing machine. White froth laces peaks of waves and streaks dark hollows of erupting water. The sand looks dull like a dirty rug cluttered with flotsam and worn thin by the wind. I walk head down and weep. My mind and heart arc the gap. I jam a huge insulator in. Why don't they realize what a waste this is? Why did I have to be in the middle of it? It's too much, too, too much. They want to play fuck-around. I'm coming in. I head for Tam Ky on Highway One.

I glimpse the brass pressure plate mid stride and launch my self over it. A shudder grabs my gut; a chill clenches my brain and Bobby flashes there in the sand as I bounce and roll into the tree line. Fuck me, motherfucker. I knew I'd be shaking later. The storm had rolled back the top layer of soft sand like peeling a blanket off a bed. I would've never seen it, probably never felt it. I drop back and loft a grenade at the mine. The grenade blows, the secondary explosion is horrendous, probably an 82 mortar round or a 105 artillery shell. Fuck. Do not drift.

I walk to Ky Phu ville, catch a ride across the river with a fisherman. Then walk the narrow road to Tam Ky, a frontier boom town. I walk from a hot area to cool. It's deserted, little flats and rises of sand dotted with spindles of pine trees and patches of cactus like ping-pong paddles sprouting in unshaded areas. I stop kicking about my 16. It's back in my bunker with the safety off.

I ask a kid in Tam Ky where I can find tuc fin, marijuana.

"Em chai co biet tuc fin o dau, khong?"

He takes me to an old man's house on a back street near the river. There's a low gate through a bramble fence. The house is bamboo and tin, carefully built. I can't tell the man's age; he's bald but smooth skinned. He gives me weak brown tea then leads me to a darkened back room.

It's cozy with a low wood-frame bed covered with grass matting. I notice the smooth block of wood with the top surface worn concave, a typical Vietnamese pillow. He sits on a low bench. Six feet and a low square table separate us. In quiet comfort I watch for the first time the exquisite, meticulous preparation for smoking opium. I get high watching this ceremony. The pipe stem is hefty dark wood about the size of a 14-inch rifle barrel. The bowl is inverted with a small hole where the opening should be. I relax more as he deftly uses a small pair of scissors to trim the wick of a burning candle.

Gradually the flame becomes a symmetrical yellow tear drop. He dips a long bristle into a small bottle of dark goo, rolling it alongside the edge of the pipe bowl, adding to it and rolling a perfect conical plug on the end of a wand. He inserts the plug into the bowl, motions me to lie on my side, then hands me the pipe, guiding the bowl over the flame. I inhale, hold, exhale. He gestures to pull deep. I watch the blue plume stream out of my lungs. Pure peace. Man, what a soothing gentle ascent. A steady quiet climb, can you punch floor 30 for me? I hand him the pipe and he smokes. I roll on my back wrapped in a soft blanket of bliss. Eleven-and-a-half months of nightmare and a dreamy respite. I'll have to tell Barr about this place.

I hitch a ride down Highway One to Chu Lai. My in-head R&R halted by an ARVN officer who refuses to give me a ride. He claims it was a "Viet Nam Jeep." I pull him out of the seat and haul him to the front of the grill. In Vietnamese I point out that Jeeps are made in America, and I will drive and he can come if he wants. I let him back in and drive off. I'd become intolerant of Vietnamese soldiers. They wouldn't fight. It made sense, though. Why should they when they had us out there taking the risk. Then the thing with the prisoners. I remember telling our sidekicks that they had crossed the line. I was going over, going to fight for the NVA.

"You'd better sky up, 'cause you're dead meat," I told them.

That's probably what got me called to the rear to see a shrink. But it felt nice to cruise down the dirt highway behind the wheel of a jeep. I felt nice again. I smile at the dude. He ignores me. The klicks fly by. I show for the appointment, whatever it was. I can't exactly remember. Twice I'd been ordered to the rear.

All those months in mountains, pleading for a rear-echelon job, now I avoid any area of military order and hierarchy. If it was the reprimand I was there for, I remember somebody coaching me on handling the officer. If it was the shrink, well, he was ordered to see me and I was ordered to see him. Neither of us knew what to make of it. He just wanted to know what it was like in the bush. He wore horned-rimmed glasses on a square face topped with thick, black hair. He knew it was a bullshit visit.

I mean, what's crazy? You gotta snap to be judged crazy. High and to the right? That's acceptable. Never come out of the bush? That's weird only in the sense that someone who hasn't been in the bush, hasn't adapted to a world steeped in working together to survive and who doesn't know different from rear-eschelon bullshit, isn't going to comprehend my preference.

He leans forward in his chair kind of awestruck and asks, "What's it like out there?"

Probably tells some good stories now. Afterwards, the first sergeant crosses my path, snatches at my shirt then backs up as I look sidelong for witnesses before cold cocking a superior. He waves his arm like a witch casting a spell and claims I'm crazy.

Chapter 44
Seven East

When Dr. Bokan walks me into the psychiatric ward on the seventh floor of the Seattle Veterans Hospital it's Fall 1999. On the ward, the nurse told me to wait in the small dining room, and Dr. Bokan wished me well and left. Suddenly, I felt very edgy, wary. The windows overlooked the Jefferson Public Golf Course, where the pro Fred Couples played as a kid.

The admission questions Dr. Bokan asked before he took me upstairs were perfunctory – birth date, height, weight, allergies to any medicine, general health. Then the last question:

"Any mental problems?" he asked.

I just start laughing. Bokan has kind of a wry manner, and this just cracks me up. I'm going into a psych ward.

He is a tall man, at least 6'5'' or 6'6", lean with a full head of close-cropped gray hair, probably in his early 50's. I'm about 5'6." As we walk the corridors, I can hardly keep up, plus I'm laughing. Every time I think about that remark, I start laughing again.

"You know, that just struck me as really funny."

I walk across the ward dining room and look down the empty hallway and then stand at the window. I feel vulnerable and have no idea what to expect, no idea what the treatment program is. I'd been attending group counseling with about four other combat vets, when the therapist noticed I'm acting overwrought, really wound tight. Plus, he'd been trying to get me to describe what a good life would be for me, what kind of future I envisioned. I tell him I'd always looked forward to someday living in the hills in a remote area with stacks of books, maybe twenty miles from a tavern and a whore house. I'd come out of the hills once a week, spend a day in the tavern, take up smoking Pall Malls again and get laid. That didn't seem like much of a life to him.

Finally, a nurse takes me to a room with four beds and goes through my shaving kit and takes away the razor. I empty my pockets and she takes my pocket knife. Then I go to a small examination room for a physical—blood pressure, temperature and so forth. The doctor palpitates my abdomen and wonders why my stomach muscles are more developed on one side than the other. I say maybe it has to do with which hand I jack off with.

Then I announce that while I'm in the hospital, I want a hearing test, physical therapy for my back and a vasectomy. He tells me that is outpatient stuff.

The patient population is a mixed bag. Some are out of it. I think they live here because they have no relatives and no place to go. Some have tried suicide. A few are homeless, but are not abusing alcohol or drugs. Some obviously have severe depression. Those cases are World War II guys.

I can't tell about the Viet Nam vets.

There is a guy in his 80's who is very depressed. He's tall and angular, and I can tell he'd once been a vibrant type guy, non-smoker, hiker type. He wears these nice walking shoes. He's trying to starve himself to death. I start sitting at his table during meals – just two of us at a small circular table. I know what he's up to. I'd watched a

75-year-old neighbor will himself to death when his wife left him. This old vet I eat with won't talk, but I'd learned he'd been a bicycle messenger as a kid in Tacoma. I ask him about the labor uprising, the Wobblies massacre in the 1930's on the 11th Street Bridge. He remembers it. He says he'd been a teacher.

I tell him I was working as a high school teacher. Every day, three times a day, I try to get him to tell me about the early days in Tacoma. I'd spent half my youth in Tacoma. At first he says he rather not talk about it. Eventually, he starts to open up a little. Soon, he's asking me if I'm going to eat my bread, drink the extra milk. I always load my tray with extra stuff. One morning I notice him walking laps around the floor. The psych ward takes half the seventh floor. He starts eating like a horse. A few days later, I watch his son check him out of the hospital.

After a couple days, I prove I'm reliable. I show up for classes and sessions with doctors on time, so I get permission to go on break with a buddy for 30 minutes off the floor. On evening break, I'd tell whoever I check out with that I'd meet them at the smoking area on time to go back up. I prowled around the hospital, since it was mostly deserted.

Being around a military establishment brings back old mannerisms and feelings. Wanting to know the area, not sleeping much, finding my way around new territory. My sixth sense comes back. I can feel a person's presence with my eyes closed and heavy background noise.

I usually go outside and sit against the wall by the huge ventilation fans with my eyes closed. This is away from the break courtyard, down a flight of stairs, on the way to the parking lot. Any time an employee walks through the area to get to the parking lot, I know they are going by. I can't hear or see them, but I'd always open my eyes and some lone person is going by.

At night I can't sleep, even on sleep medication. I'd go into the visitor's area and move a couple of stuffed chairs into a sort of chaise lounge and stare out at the lights of downtown Seattle. I close the door and play the boom box low on classical music. Nurse Marilyn finds me there. She'd been a Navy psych nurse for twenty years. She'd stop by for a few minutes and we'd talk.

She did more to help me sort things out than the sessions with a psychiatrist and resident shrinks from the University of Washington. I'd hidden pillows and a blanket in the game cabinet and after a few days, I found fresh pillows and a clean blanket there.

They have patient government, which was another exercise in being responsible and participating in society. We also have little jobs we have to do, like setting up the dining room for meals, cleaning the pantry – my job – or waking up patients in the morning.

Patient government is like student government and you know what job I wanted – yeah, president. When the cycle for new officers comes around, one of the younger patients asks, "Do you want to be president? I'll nominate you." He's a black dude with a shaved head and an attitude. He wants to be bad news, like Richard Roundtree in the movie *Shaft*. There is a problem with my nomination. I'd come back from break late the day of elections. So I'm busted and my privileges, including running for office, are suspended until 5:30 p.m. It means I can't be nominated for office. There's a new nurse on duty that day.

Patient government convenes a special session for

elections at five that evening. When it comes time for nominations, I'm preparing my little speech for declining; But then, the nomination for president happens minutes after 5:30 p.m. and I'm eligible.

I get the job and hand pick the officers I want, including Shaft. But then I almost blow it again. When they finished the election, I went up to the acting president to take the gavel. He'd been elected as a prank by somebody who knew the guy couldn't read well and didn't know what was up. I wanted to save him from further embarrassment, but he didn't understand what I was trying to do. So when I went up to take over the meeting, the new nurse thinks I'm harassing the guy, being aggressive, and she writes me up. Busted again.

The next evening, nurse Marilyn tells me I probably won't be able to be president because I'd been written up. I explain things, and she takes care of it so I'm president of Seven East Psychiatric Ward, after all.

I'd covered state legislative committee hearings for a job I had, so I know how to run meetings. I rule with an iron hand, no discussion of issues from the floor. The quicker we get through the meetings, the quicker we get on break.

There was talk of a coup d'etat when I dumped a whole drawer of sugar packets while organizing the pantry during my daily duty. The drawer was labeled "crackers" and I didn't have any use for sugar, so I dumped all of it. That upset the junkies who craved sugar. At the next meeting, I donated a box of sugar cubes I'd found in an employee break room downstairs on one of my forays. I also found a phone I could get an outside line on for free long distance phone calls.

I'm starting to get kind of wound up from being around a military establishment and other Viet Nam veterans. The Seattle Police bring one to the ward in handcuffs late one night. He's wearing camouflaged utilities and face paint. He'd been a Marine door gunner in I-Corps in 1968. He was working as a carpenter framing on a condominium project. That day the project manager got on his case about not going fast enough. So, that night he snuck on to the project and started dismantling a wing he'd been framing. He liked the way I controlled the patient government meetings and even saluted me one morning.

My therapy sessions are not too interesting, but I get plenty of attention. When I met with my team, we take over the break room and the psychiatrist, psychiatric internists, psychologists and their interns form a semi-circle around the chair I sat in. They are impressed that I learned all seven of their names.

Their questions are geared toward assessing my reaction to medication which is supposed to stabilize my tendency to get wound up. Apparently, I come across as not only hyper vigilant, but hyper in general. Sleep deprivation contributes to that.

I get a half-day pass and borrow Shaft's late-model Mustang to go visit my son. It's a beautiful, sunny October Saturday, and I take him to a private dock we have permission to fish from on Lake Washington. It belongs to the neighbor of a friend of my son's. I lie on my back in the sun, which feels good on an old back injury that has flared up. I ask him about the finger he injured at the playground at his middle school. "Did you ever get it X-rayed?"

"No. Ken looked at it and felt it and pulled on it and said it would be okay."

Ken is his soccer coach and an orthopedic surgeon. I know he is a little overzealous about winning. I knew he wouldn't want Cole to miss any games, since he was one of the leading scorers and solid defensive player.

"Does it still hurt?" I ask Cole.

"Yeah. I told Ken it hurts."

"Let me see it," I say.

It had happened 10 days earlier. He had told me about it during a phone call. His finger is very swollen and discolored.

"You need an X-ray," I say.

I'm due back at the hospital at 6 p.m., and it's already late afternoon. The x-ray shows a broken pinky finger right at the growth plate.

"If we don't treat this, your finger will grow into a tight curl," the emergency room doctor explained.

She carefully shows us the X-ray of the injury and compares it to an x-ray she'd taken of his uninjured hand.

Bad call, coach. I'm irate. After she treats it, I have to hurry him home and then race the clock to get back to the ward on time. But in a Mustang, that turned out to be kind of fun.

At the end of the two week evaluation period, the shrinks think about having me go through the two-week posttraumatic stress treatment program, but realize that being in an environment with only Viet Nam vets is not a good idea. I agree. I get discharged with a sack full of mood controlling medicine and sleep medication. The side affects are enough to motivate me to find my own ways to stay calm or keep from going off the deep end or wherever they thought I was headed. After a year or so, I'm able to reduce the dosage on both.

If anyone knew where I was or where I needed to go it was nurse Marilyn, who shook her head one day and asked, “When are you going to come home?”

Chapter 45
A Day in the Rear

I make it out of Tam Ky without any more trouble about Jeep ownership and made it to Chu Lai and talk to the shrink. I hung out for a day with my old radioman, Arnold, one of the three originals of our rebel band. We sat on a bench on a patch of hard-baked, red dirt outside a supply Quonset hut. I was sitting there before Arnold met me after chow. A big, black sergeant came all brisk and starched up. He had a couple guys who were in transit with him. He told me to get off my ass and go on garbage detail with the two. He was definitely a lifer, all squared away. Hardcore.

"I don't do garbage details," I smirk.

He gets all puffed up and says, "I'll jump in your shit with both feet." His eyes-bugged-pogue-bad-ass-routine, and he says, "You don't say shit when I assign duty, you got that straight? What's your goddam' name, boy?"

This rear-eschelon bullshit kicks me into the "eat the apple, fuck the corps" mode. "Well," (pause) my name ain't Roy (pause]) and I'm from 1-1-6."

His shoulders drop slightly as he searches for some way to change course.

"Git the fuck on," he glares at the two standing by, spins on his heel and starts shouting orders over their heads.

Arnold strolls up and sits down next to me.

"I'm fighting a fucking war out there," I said, "and

some dude tells me to pick up garbage,"

"And?"

"I said nah, I don't feel like it and he starts up and wants to know what outfit I'm with and so on, and I tell him and he backs off."

Arnold nods his head.

"Yeah, the word back here is don't fuck with anybody from six. Plus everybody back here thinks you're psycho."

"There it is," and held my fist out to dap (a form of hand greeting) with him.

"It's a bitch back here," he says as we bump fists, top and bottom, side to side.

"I broke out in hives for the first two weeks I was back here. They won't let me back out with you guys."

We are the first ones in the mess hall the next morning. Another ramshackle Quonset hut, the pea-green linoleum floor still streaked from mopping. Just us and the cook who never said a word.

Rockets start coming in. Arnold and I are reading them, timing them. We look at each other. Do we have a solid copy on this? Who's going to make a move? They are walking toward us from the chopper pad. They're within range, each one a little closer, coming our way.

We get up from the table to get on the deck. I look around for a dry spot but I can't find one that I wouldn't have to contort around like a pretzel so I go back to the table. Fuck it.

The freight train screeches and crashes into a barracks about 30 meters from the mess hall. Four guys killed. Killed in action. Too much action last night, more likely. Too hung over to notice; probably too tuned out from beer, weed and young Asian muff to know incoming from an outbound jet.

The food is okay, at least not straight from a can. But I need to get away from the bullshit and out where I'm on my own, can run the war my way. I catch a chopper back to the Army base at Tam Ky. I visit the old man again. I check his ID – 52years old. He looks good, smooth. I thought opium was supposed to cause physical deterioration. Turn you into a sack of bones. I'd ask our doc what he knows about poppy.

Chapter 46
Finding Another Edge on R&R

The stewardess bursts into tears when I board the plane. It's a chartered flight from Sydney back to Da Nang with the same crew that flew us to Sydney. Exhausted and wound tighter than thread wrapped around a homemade tattoo needle. I met her on the flight to Sydney. She's a slim blond who dropped out of Stanford. On the first flight, I spend much of the flight in the stews' small seating compartment joking and flirting with her. I remember we talked about weed. She'd given me an address in the the Bay Area after I told her I'd send her some opium treated joints.

"We hardly ever get any, 'cuz we're way out in the boonies," I explain.

"But if one of our team gets back to the rear area he'll buy a pack of five rolled joints in a sealed plastic bag. They're big," I said as I held my forefingers about 4 inches apart.

Going to Sydney after 12 months is like going from one planet to another. I avoid Kings Cross, where the other GIs, and the hookers hang out. There is so much new stimulus – not jungle, hills, and death. I become frenetic, roaming the city day and night. I don't drink or party or get high. I get laid once. That's it. When I get on the return plane, I guess I look crazed. That's when the stewardess burst out crying. I'm out of it. The stews have me sit in their compartment the whole flight back. I think one was with me at all times. They gave me a pill, a tranquilizer, I guess. When the flight lands in Da Nang, the captain sees me off. He's a jolly guy with a big mustache wearing shorts and knee socks.

"You flew this plane?"

"Yep. You escaped death again," he chuckles and hands me a big cigar.

Outside the airstrip in Da Nang, I stand at a teeming intersection. I set my little duffel bag down, drop my guard for just a second. Civilians gather around me trying to distract me while a young guy grabs my bag and jumps on the back of a motorbike. Pretty slick. Only it was too congested to make a clean getaway and I jerk the guy off the back of the motorbike as it roars off. I have my bag back with one hand and the thief by the throat with the other. I'm talking some strongly-worded Vietnamese when three Air Force MPs step in. You don't speak harshly to Vietnamese, much less grab one by the throat.

In the jeep on the way to their base, I tell them what happened. They're really calm, really decent. They take me to their mess hall, which is unbelievable. There's three cooks and wonderful food. There's a salad bar, different entrees, several kinds of dessert and machines dispensing cold milk, white and chocolate. Unbelievable. I eat as much as I can.

"Could you get me a supply of vitamins?" I ask.

"What for?"

"My guys. All we eat are C-rations and sometimes not even that – just what we might get from villagers in a hamlet."

I guess they figure there was no way to abuse vitamins. They round up a couple of bottles.

"Ah, you know, sorry to tell you this, but we have

to turn you over to Marine MPs."

At the Marine base near China Beach, they drop me in front of a two-story plywood shack with a Conex cargo container next to it and a cell just inside the doorway of the building.

A pogue in a white T-shirt and an attitude starts questioning me, handing me a ration of shit.

"Fuck you, I'm not dealing with a dipshit pogue."

"You better shape up boy," he says.

"My name's not Roy," I said, taking up the challenge.

He flies from behind his typewriter and two others grab my arms.

"Hey, I've got a five-year-old brother that can kick your pogue ass," I sneer.

I let them shove me out the door toward the Conex box. When one of the guards swings the door open, I fling the one on my right onto his face into the box and slam the door on his ankle. Suddenly I'm surrounded by four guys pointing dusty M-16s at me.

Hilarious. Pogues with weapons. Back inside the barren office I tell them I'll only talk to the man in charge. While I wait for their next move, I hand my new pack of Pall Malls and some matches to the prisoners in the cell. They're packed in there tight. Then a burly guy in a white T-shirt and black eye comes down the stairs to deal with me. Obviously not an officer.

"I'm only talking to the officer in charge."

"Why don't you talk to me?

"You're not the head pogue here."

"What's up man?" A prisoner grins. "Where you from dude?"

After a bit, a guard leads me upstairs and I walk into a dim office where a tired-looking captain sits behind a desk. He asks for my name, rank, serial number.

"What outfit are you with."

"CAP One, one six."

I doubt he'd heard of it, but our team had been on the tally board at this very base with most kills, captures, captured weapons and intell during one six-week period.

"Have you ever been wounded?"

"Yes."

"Where?"

"In the head."

He blanches and I grin, realizing how that may be interpreted.

"Well, what do you want?" he says softly.

"Off this base and back in the bush."

"Well okay."

He walks downstairs with me. As I walk out the door the prisoners are yelling and cheering.

"Hey man. Are you a prisoner, or what?"

Chapter 47
Leadership

After ten months in the bush, I get busted. I wasn't caught doing anything wrong like shooting heroin—I didn't even know there was heroin in Viet Nam until I read about it after I got home in the Spring of 1969. I get busted for being a maverick, for operating unsupervised. I think I may have rubbed people the wrong way for doing things that PFCs and Lance Corporals don't do, like going up with spotter pilots, or being invited to sit with a Vietnamese general at a celebration in a ville that we were just supposed to be at for security. Maybe the E-6 sitting across from me didn't think I belong at the table laughing and joking in Vietnamese. Maybe the REMFs think I'm laughing at them. Maybe it's just on account of my attitude.

Occasionally, I'd get remarks from lifers in the rear like, "When did you make Lieutenant Colonel?" I'd call headquarters on the radio to tell them some plan we cooked up or about an operation we were planning with an army infantry unit. Sometimes the rank designation on mail I received from home was crossed out and replaced with "Junior General."

Anyway, I get a call on the radio one day informing me I'd been busted.

"Hey Akins, how does it feel to be back at E-2?"

After 10 months of combat and 30 days of language school, I'd made E-3. Not bad, I'd been an E-2 with almost a year of combat. I mean, you come out of 12 weeks of boot camp as an E-1.

Rank, medals, even R&R was not something I was concerned with. The military was not going to be my career. This was a pretty common attitude that developed with the guys who were grinding out 13-month tours in the thick of it. The command people had it figured out though.

The Command Chronologies for 1st CAG in December 1968 note a problem in leadership. The report describes how the average number of men in a CAP is well below Tactical Operation.

The only other problem was that at the end of the reporting period nine CAPS had corporals, (E-4 in rank), for squad leaders instead of sergeants (E-5) as Tactical Operations provide. The report goes on to say that:

"Particularly in the case of private first class, the difficulty in being promoted to lance corporal is a significant factor in career motivation within 1st CAG."

Too many PFCs and less than 12 promotions per month. Guess who scarfs up any available openings? The troopees who handle the paperwork for promotions, that's who.

In the last small team I was with, CAP 1-1-6, we were a bunch of misfits who could handle the bush and were quite effective. Our team was at the top of the "board" for kills, captures, captured weapons and intelligence gathered for a couple of months. It was a hot area and we knew what we were doing.

Leadership in the bush sometimes starts out with people in place according to the box and arrow diagrams you find in college textbooks, but real leadership sort of evolves, especially in the smaller units where tactics are important and everybody can handle all the responsibilities that go with running combat missions. The Combined Action Platoon teams that I ended up with after Khe Sanh folded were groups of five to eight Marines led by a squad leader. According the the tactical operations diagrams, he was supposed to be a sergeant, an E-5 in rank.

The first time I saw someone at a CAP who was an E-5, he had come to take over. Headquarters didn't know what they had going. They never came out there. I'd been with three CAPs and only one had as high a rank as corporal for a squad leader. He's the one who collected fingers and ears and ordered one-piece polyester leisure suits.

The other time was when headquarters decided we needed someone in charge of CAP 1-1-6. We were all private first class and one E-3 or lance corporal.

After three months of kicking ass, after helping plan an operation for an army infantry company; after advising a Seal Team insertion operation; after flying with a spotter pilot who called in six jets and got the best bomb damage assessment of the day for I-Corps; after relocating civilians from a free fire zone to a secure ville south of us – they decided to put somebody in charge. I didn't like that.

This new CAP commander was a good guy. I'd met him way back in the first team I was assigned to. He was a sergeant with two tours, a squared away Marine. We were squared away in a different way, in being able to count on each other, in knowing what to do when the shit hit the fan. For him leadership was by the book. He didn't like our clothes – cut off jean jacket, shorts made from a red nylon mail bag, some polka-dot pajama bottoms made by a girl in Ky Phu ville, sunglasses, mustaches. He didn't like our attitude. Having someone in charge didn't sit well with us, because he was going to demonstrate who was "in charge."

His way was not our way. The thing was, I knew this guy. We hit it off when we were both in 1-1-1 and he was just part of the team. But he'd changed, all serious and shit.

They must have told him that our shit was raggedy and we needed to be squared away. The last straw was when he ordered two of us to swim in from a swift boat one night after we'd spent the evening patrolling along the coast. Within a week or so, our new leader was gone, transferred at the request of the Vietnamese side.

When I think about it, we didn't consider ourselves a Marine outfit. We were beyond that. We were jungle fighters. We didn't have much connection with the Marine Corps.

I had two encounters with the military establishment that caught me off guard. An officer at our Chu Lai headquarters reprimanded me:

"Hey, you. Don't you salute an officer?"

"Ah nooo. I thought it was not supposed to be a good idea in a war zone."

"What branch are you with soldier?" he barked.

I actually had to think for a second. Ah, may-rine? I'd forgotten about what branch I was part of. I could hardly pronounce the word "Marine." It was a wake up. I stood there thinking, I've forgotten what the fuck I was. And I forgot how to salute. I started snapping up both hands. He was getting red in the face.

Inside the PX this boot-looking guy, a lieutenant with single gold bars on his collar was looking at some Brasso, the liquid we used in boot camp to shine brass belt buckles, buttons and I forget what else.

"Will I need some of this?" he asked.

I took it from him and looked at the small print on the label.

"Nah, I don't think you can get high on this stuff."

He looked at me weird and then I realized that he had just gotten here.

I just preferred being in the bush, especially out at 1-1-6. Plenty remote.

Once we established 1-1-6 we could run the war our way. We were all experienced bush rats. By now I had that sixth sense and could sometimes "feel" the presence of enemy. I'd become like Miller and White.

We were patrolling one night, soon after six formed up. The water rumbles in. A steady breeze pushes me along. Was that a jog in the tree line ahead or not? We'd been hit one night about here. At the time, I noticed the jut in the tree line and how it bent toward the beach before we got up to it.

There is no starlight this night, a perfect night for sneakin' and peekin'. We'd gone about one-and-half klicks when I felt the gut check. I just knew gooks were there. Barr is behind me. Arnold, Muledick and Ichabod, who is carrying the radio, are strung out behind him. I slip back to Barr.

"See that little jag in the tree line about 100 meters up?"

"What do ya think, man?" he whispers as he takes the machine gun off his shoulder.

"I think we're going to get hit."

I wave Muledick up.

"Link up about three-hundred rounds and assist for Barr. When I move out, get about 30 meters behind and be ready to rock. If they see me, they might not notice you further back. I'm going to get an on-call fire mission set up and then we'll move out."

I move down the line passing the word to Arnold and Ichabod. "Gimme the handset Ick," I said. "There's a little point up ahead. I want an on call for some 105s for it."

We'd been getting excellent artillery fire from the battery near the town of Tam Ky. We always went out after hitting a spot and I'd call the battery and tell them any results or how they did on hitting the spots. They really dug that. A battery could be up to five miles away, so they wouldn't even know what the territory they were firing on looked like. I'd call back a report on what we found, bodies, blood trails or bunkers that had taken a direct hit. They were pretty appreciative and liked working for us.

Thirty years later when I visited the war museum in Saigon, there were a set of 105 mm and 155 mm artillery pieces side-by-side on the museum grounds. I got giddy when I saw them; they had been life savers. The trick to getting artillery quick and on-the-money was to call in clear and concise missions, never extraneous shit like "we need some help here, they're all around us." Just straight dope.

"Redhawk, this is Badnews, over."

"This is Redhawk, go."

"Fire mission. On call HE. Grid Golf Hotel eight, four four, niner, six, five. Code name Extra. How copy, over?"

"Roger, I have solid copy for On call fire mission Extra. HE on GH eight, four four, niner, six, five, one. over."

"Roger that. It's fire for effect and a repeat. Badnews out."

"Roger. Redhawk out."

"Okay." I tell our radioman. "All set. If the shit hits, call Redhawk for code name Extra. If it happens, fan out and fire."

When I walk by Muledick, he has every belt we have with us linked up and a grin. The belt went from the gun, now in Barr's two hands, in a nice loop to Muledick's shoulder and down his back almost to the ground. He has his M-79 slung on his right shoulder and is putting two rounds each in both chest pockets.

I get about 30 meters ahead and we move out. Just as I get near the jag in the tree line, we get hit with automatic weapons fire. Barr cuts loose and I'm firing and rolling. Ichabod calls for the fire mission. Within seconds rounds are walking up the beach just in the tree line. After that initial burst they aren't firing anymore. Barr and Muledick have so much lead and death flying into the tree line, the fire fight is over after their first burst.

We move into the tree line, set up for a few minutes, hear nothing then move out down the beach for 10 minutes, then double back and move past the spot where they had opened up on us. The rest of the night is quiet.

At first light we find one good-sized patch of bloody sand and part of a hand. We stick around just long enough to call in a sit rep to the battery.

"Redhawk, Redhawk this is Bad News, over."

"This is Redhawk, go."

"Roger, ah they hit us with automatic fire at the spot you were targeted for fire mission Extra. Be advised your rounds nipped it in the bud. One bad guy is out of commission for a while, maybe the duration. Your shots were right on the money, thank you, over."

"Roger, anytime, any place. You call, they fall, out."

I don't think I'd had any squad leaders, infantry or CAG that I really got along with. The early going with Echo 2/1 was okay at times. I didn't get to know any officers. In infantry, the officers tend to stay further back in the column.

Actually, I guess I saw three officers, since doctors were officers. One morning at Khe Sanh I couldn't stand up straight from pain in my abdomen and back. I went to the hospital bunker where the doc gave me a digital rectal exam and proclaimed that I had prostatitis.

"What's that?"

"That's what old men like the Pope get. Have you been drinking lots of water?"

Right. For months we carried three canteens but never knew when we would come across a stream to refill them. So, I practiced water conservation. Take one sip, swallow it; take another sip and spit it back into the canteen. Often, when I did come across a stream during our hump to Khe Sanh, I'd have nearly full canteens.

I had to stay back while my platoon went out on mine sweep duty outside the wire. It was May 19, Ho Chi Minh's birthday. They were ambushed and everyone in my squad was killed or wounded.

The aftermath of surviving combat is that you take home some things you learned. Your sixth sense is alive and well, sometimes dormant but always kicking in under certain stimuli or triggers. Your lack of fear, your cool under fire, come in handy for serious accidents or criminal attacks, such as the time five guys tried to break into my girlfriend's house. That near rape got me revved into the combat mode. It never occurred to me to call the cops.

Chapter 48
Aftermath

Trying on the American Dream again is not easy, because supervisors can't tolerate the mistakes that veterans might make. They can't put up with guys who are unsafe on construction jobs, or can't play petty politics on the job or in the offices. Combat takes away who you were and makes you who you are – a misfit whose American Dream has been shattered.

Construction jobs are temporary anyway, and you can bounce around, quit or get fired and go from job-to-job, until you burn too many bridges and run out of contractors. I got black-balled by a contractor for raising hell about safety issues. I had learned to get the job done my way. It was hard for me to work with too much dumb supervision.

I tried working as a fireman, but discovered it was a quasi-military organization with captains and lieutenants and all the ass-kissing and back stabbing. I worked with a woman who was incapacitated by any volume of smoke that amounted to more than that from the head of a match; who couldn't pick a pack of hose off an engine truck, who couldn't pick a person off the floor and carry them across a room.

I worked with a lieutenant who wanted to write me up because I was already in a building with a hose calling for water, while everybody else was still fumbling around with gear and deciding how to enter the building.

The kind of teamwork expected of me in civilian life was very different from the kind I had gotten used to in military combat. While bouncing around, changing careers, I found a good white collar job – communications director for the Washington Conservation Commission. The job was not civil service; it was funded by grant money, a tobacco tax dedicated to natural resource protection. I interviewed well and took the offer.

No more commuting 60 miles one-way, climbing towers and wiring stuff on a container crane in a port city. The office was small, eight people, each one in charge of a program. I was the minister of propaganda for a worthwhile cause and working with salt of the earth people, farmers and ranchers involved in a grassroots, statewide, voluntary network dedicated to natural resource conservation. My boss was a gem.

"You're the pro," he said. "Do what you think needs to be done. If I think of anything, I'll let you know."

"Can I work flextime?" I said.

"Sure. The governor just sent a memo encouraging flextime and working out of your home, especially commuters."

Perfect. Just perfect for my kind of independent style, with no supervision to speak of. The crew was great; everybody but one guy that got kicked out of the field because nobody could stand working with him. So I was unencumbered by anything. When I was asked to run a joint public-relations education program with a big state resource agency – Fish and Game department, I figured out what we needed to do. Design the program and all the stuff we'd need to encourage landowners to set aside land for wildlife habitat. I put together the marketing pieces and a media packet and went to the public affairs office of Fish and Game. They had a crew. Graphic artists, writers, editors, photographer, radio and TV guy – the works. And they had their own print shop.

I talked with the staff honcho, a sharp, former newspaperman who had covered natural resource issues for a large daily. He liked the plan and set up a meeting with me and the people he assigned to the task. That went fine, except I realized they figured something like this would take months. The graphic artist was on vacation, the writers figured they could turn out some copy in a month, and so on. I figured a week or two and the materials would be printed and mailed statewide.

"Do you have a logo for your agency," I asked, already scheming on how to end-run all this bullshit.

"Yes."

"Give me a camera-ready of it."

I asked the staff honcho what the director wanted to say about the program, and suggested that we should have a joint cover letter from both our directors.

"Is Curt in the building today?" I asked.

"Yes. He's here just this morning and then he meets with the governor's staff all afternoon," I was told.

"Good."

"But he's tied up all morning."

Once I got that letter, I could build all the other stuff – fact sheets, brochures, award certificates and a how-to guide for the farmers and ranchers to participate in the wildlife habitat promotion, along with a generic press release for their local media. I wrote the script for a radio spot. Since their agency had their own print shop, we wouldn't get bogged down in the state print shop process, which did the printing for all the state agencies and the legislature. Once I got the joint letter approved by Fish and

Games's public affairs director, I wouldn't need anything from his people. I built everything in a week or two. The radio spots were in the can. All I needed was the Fish and Game director's signature and we would be ready to print and mail statewide. When I called their director's office I got the run-around for two days.

I got the camera-ready letter and drove across town to their building. His receptionist had never seen me. But I'd run into Curt running during lunch time a couple times. A circuit around the lake near the capital campus made a nice five-mile run route. He was known as very savvy, very independent, and not worried about butting heads with big powerful special interests groups. The media dubbed him a maverick. My kind of guy. I greeted his secretary at her desk outside his office

"Hi, I'm John Akins, working on a joint project with Fish and Game and need Curt's signature on this letter.

"I'm sorry he's not available," she said.

"Is he in the building?"

"Yes, but he's busy at the moment."

His office door was open. I took a couple of steps to one side and saw him working at his desk. I kept right on going.

"You can't go in there," she said, coming out of her chair.

"Hi, Curt," I said. "I've got the wildlife habitat project materials ready for the project that the Conservation Commission is doing with Fish and Game. I just need your signature on the joint cover letter."

"Oh, oh, ah good."

"Just need your signature under your name here and

everything is all set. Should be mailed statewide next week."

"Fine. Ah, how are doing, still running?"

"Yep. Gotta' run now. Thanks for letting me interrupt. This is the last thing. I'll make a copy and leave it with your secretary."

I walked to the secretary's desk. "I need to make a copy of this to leave here," I said.

"We don't have a copy machine here," she said.

"No sweat. I'll find one around here somewhere." I had all the camera-ready stuff in my car, went and got it and took it to the Fish and Game communications office.

"Here's the joint wildlife habitat project," I said, "and the labels for our mailing list and labels for all the newspapers, radio and TV stations statewide."

The assistant communications director looked real startled. "But we haven't done any work on it, except for the director's message on the cover letter."

"Everything your boss and I talked about is all here," I said "and the radio spot is set to run. All you need to do is get this to your print shop. If you fill out the print order and tell me where the shop is, I'll drop it off."

She looked a little confused as she filled out the print request form and handed it to me.

It was easy for me to bypass the queen bees and drones from another agency, but operating this way when I worked for Labor and Industries or the Office of the Superintendent of Public Instruction usually raised a shit storm. I'd usually end up leaving or getting told, "Some people just aren't cut out for this kind of job."

It turned out that most people in the system were disturbed by my way of doing things. I had to tell them I was on a special mission or I had to go directly to people higher up. But sometimes this created problems. My boss was concerned about the manner in which I talked to one legislator. I reminded her that the issue was important to her district and that now was not the time to throw a monkey wrench into the works. I may have been a little too forceful after doing all the work and then having her waffle on about it.

She was a vice-chairman of the committee but didn't know that she was the prime sponsor of the bill under discussion and had to be reminded of that by the chairman when a second was needed to pass the thing out of committee. She was also someone who would leave town around noon Fridays, skipping her committee hearing, maybe even an occasional vote on the floor when the House was in session because she had to beat the traffic to be home for dinner with her husband. I really didn't have a lot of patience with someone who wasn't too on the ball and not too committed.

As soon as I was called on the carpet by my boss, who couldn't take the heat when the representative complained, I went to the Speaker's office and Majority Floor leader's office to tell them that I was quitting.

"No, no wait," the speaker said as I handed him and his colleague my resignation letter. We can take care of you," he said. We put you in a bad situation. You shouldn't quit. We can take care of you; we put you in a bad situation."

"It's a done deal," I said, and went home to tell my wife who had quit her job to be a full-time mother for a year when our son was born six months earlier.

I'm an active job searcher and went to work for the

Superintendent of Public Instruction, putting out their crappy eight-page newsletter and doing media relations. They were still building the newsletter the way it was done during the stone ages – sending out hard copy to be type set, then cutting and pasting up blue-line galleys. Desktop publishing would have been a lot cheaper.

A former career army public affairs guy worked in the office but was way underemployed. He answered the phone and did only what his job description called for, which had little to do with putting out any product. I'd been upstairs, interviewing department heads for the newsletter and saw new Macintosh computers, perfect for desktop publishing, being unpacked here and there. Why didn't we have one?

My boss had no training or experience in the kind of work we did. She had been a girlfriend of the number two guy in the agency and was very suspicious of my idea. She said our budget was tighter than other departments. I went to the agency comptroller, got the figures for putting out the newsletter, and told him how desktop publishing could eliminate all but the printing costs and cut the man-hours drastically.

"Well," he said, "if you're trying to justify buying a new computer you're going about it the right way. You would save the agency thousands of dollars every quarter. But if Charlotte doesn't want it, you won't get it. She's got a lot of power in this agency."

"This will make her look good," I said. "Saving money and man-hours?"

I talked to Stan, my co-worker about how we could turn this operation around.

"I'm going to have Charlotte come downstairs and

I'll lay this all out for her. We'll have control of the whole operation in-house, which will be more efficient and save time. You can back me up, right?"

"Yeah," said Stan.

She came down to the basement for the meeting. The three of us sat at a table together and I laid out the cost savings and efficiency thing.

Charlotte said "No! This is the way we've always done it."

I couldn't convince her and Stan never said a word.

Charlotte said "drop it" and left.

"I thought you were going to back me up?" I said to Stan.

"I need to keep this job," he said. "I'm in the civil service system, and in ten more years I can retire."

A couple days later she popped into our basement office all huffy and sternly told me to stop working with the comptroller on operating costs for our office.

"I'm just working behind the scenes to improve things here," I said. "I don't want any glory or credit. I can make you look good."

"No," she said, "and I don't want to see you out of the office. There's no need for you to leave your desk to wander around the building talking to people."

"I interview people," I said. "I am trying to put some human interest in our rag. Nobody reads it. It's dense, solid copy on regulations and reports of board meetings. We can send that stuff out in a separate fold-in."

"Go back to your desk," she said.

I wandered around awhile and dropped in on the graphic designer and the personnel director, two guys I knew were jake. I talked about my problem with Charlotte.

"Hey, I gave up years ago," said the graphic designer. "I tried so many times to fix that layout, but no way. Not with Charlotte."

I told the personnel director our newsletter was an embarrassment to the agency and cost way too much money, and I was unable to do anything about it.

"I know," he said. "Charlotte is one of the biggest problems in this agency, but she's connected with leadership. She's got power."

I had eleven days vacation time on the books, most of it accrued from my time in the communications office at the legislature. I was going to Hawaii to do the Ironman Triathlon. Charlotte hadn't initialed the payroll form I had to submit when you take a vacation. Stan told me she never let anybody take more than two or three days at a time. I went up to payroll and told them I didn't have the form signed yet.

"Oh, you work for Charlotte, don't you?" she chuckled.

"Yeah, I just wanted to let you know the dates I'd be gone, in case I don't have the form for you."

It was getting close. I went into Charlotte's office to ask her for the form. She couldn't find it. I could see it in the clutter on her desk, two or three circles of coffee stain on it. I picked it up off her desk. "Is this it?" I said.

She started to complain about the block of time I wanted.

"I've got the next newsletter in the can," I said, "and everything else is taken care of ready to go to the printer. Stan's hip to what has to be done. I'm leaving Oct. 17 and I'll be back on the 28th."

"I'll think about it," she said.

I wanted to quit by telegram from Kona, Hawaii. It really struck me as a novel idea, but my wife talked me out of it. It had been the worst six-months of work I'd ever put in. When I got back from the trip, the secretary in our office was leaving in a couple weeks, moving to Las Vegas with her husband.

"I'm so glad to get out of here," she beamed. "I'm going to miss you though. It's been fun watching you stand up to Charlotte. Everyone's so afraid of her, and she's such a bitch."

"Careful now," I said. "Did you get your letter of recommendation? The walls have ears."

Roberts, in legal across the hallway, was one of Charlotte's loyal spies.Two days later Charlotte called me into her office.

"You know your six-month's probation is just about up," she said, "and I don't think you're going to make it."

She was flipping through a thick file folder. I could see the borders of holes on the old-style computer paper. She had a file of blank computer paper.

"I've been documenting things where you're deficient," she said.

"Oh," I said. "Should I go get somebody from personnel to be with us for this review? Should I get a union rep in here? What do you have in the file? Maybe we should go over it."

"I don't need to show you anything."

"Charlotte," I laughed, standing. "You've got a file full of blank paper. You don't even know how to fire somebody."

My wife, son and I were sharing a house with a

friend of my wife's. She had the downstairs master bedroom off the rec room. We had the two bedrooms upstairs. We shared the rest. Our baby had his own room.

While I was pounding the pavement after getting smoked by Charlotte, my wife's friend, a lawyer in her mid-thirties was advising my wife that I was not "supporting" her, that I was only thinking of myself, not willing to sacrifice. This woman also didn't like me typing resumes and cover letters after 8 p.m., which was her bedtime. The kitchen table was above her bedroom, so I went to the far end of the basement, put the typewriter on a folded beach towel on the floor and worked hunched over on my knees.

One night my wife comes downstairs after a few hours at the kitchen table with our housemate and starts getting hysterical about us not having an income. I couldn't figure out what she was worried about. I mean I put her through two-and-a-half years of college and bought a house and took her to her sister's third wedding in Hawaii and managed to invest at least 15 percent of just about every paycheck for years.

I was forty-one years old. I was used to finding work even while changing careers just about every three or four years. I couldn't figure out what she was worried about. I'd always kept a cash flow going.

In the morning I drove 60 miles to the electrical hiring hall and took a two-week call wiring on a crane in the Port of Seattle. I marked exempt on my federal income tax W-2 form and took home a weekly paycheck at $23 an hour with no deductions. Then I resumed my job search and two months later went to work in the public affairs office of the Department of Labor and Industries. My boss had been a reporter and guild officer at the Tacoma News Tribune daily newspaper and had been smoked when new owners busted the union.

"We should be able to get you back-doored into civil service," he said, "when this slot gets changed to permanent, which has to happen to keep up with the workload. We've got projects that have been hanging for six months."

I worked with a couple of other Tribune reporters who had crossed over and become flacks and they were pros. I was running at lunch with the agency's legal counsel and looking forward to getting into civil service, where it's really pretty difficult to get smoked unless you're embezzling or doing drugs on the job, and then it takes a long time to happen and you're getting paid all the while you're off the job and so on. My boss had to get one of his cronies into the system ahead of me and then my slot would be next. I hadn't learned to kiss ass yet, but I was getting the hang of smoozing a little, like asking the agency director how the speech I wrote for him went.

"You worked on that speech?" he said. "I thought Jim did all my speeches."

"Yeah, I'm John Akins. I work for Jim. "He got in a bind. Did you like the joke I threw in there? Someone told me you'd spent summers digging in the dirt while you were in college."

"Yeah, it worked pretty well."

"Good, good. Well I gotta get to it. The budget guys are behind schedule on that report for the legislature. Jim asked me to help on that, too."

Blatant ass kissing, I thought to myself as I walked on. I got the hang of the hierarchy and only angled around one department head who wanted to get her paw prints on a brochure I was writing. She was questioning the layout and thought she had some insight on the graphic design. Our graphic designer was good, and he was fast, and he was an ex-Marine. The layout sat on the program director's desk for a couple days, even after I left a note and some phone messages. So I left another note.

I ran into Joe, the agency director, and he asked me what I was doing, so I showed him the dummy on the brochure, and he liked the layout and asked when it was going to the printer and how long that would take.

"It's at the printer now," I said. "Thanks for your suggestions."

Chapter 49
Babysitting

I never learned the tricks of shining on officers or guys that out-ranked me. I just never had much contact with them. In the military, I shared what I knew or whatever I did. I didn't treat information like a lever to gain advantage. I could show a spotter-pilot targets. I could tell Army captains or Navy commanders what they would find if they wanted to run a patrol in our area of operation. I didn't worry about pleasing the hierarchy in the rear with the gear. Jealousy and backbiting just were not part of life in the bush, and that's one reason I came to prefer the bush.

The headquarters contingent came to a secure ville in our area to celebrate some awards ceremony with their Viet Namese counterparts. I can't remember the occasion, even though there are pictures of me sitting at the banquet table. There's a picture of me looking at a motorbike. I can guess what I was thinking – if it belonged to an American or to the Red Cross, how could I steal it? How could we make use of it. We could use it on a two-man killer team patrol. Push it along with us at night and make a quick get-away when the shit got too hot.

I don't remember the Vietnamese forces standing in formations, or the all-woman Popular Force company dressed in crisp, black uniforms and toting shotguns. I remember a staff sergeant from headquarters glowering across the table at me because I was there and I wasn't part of headquarters and didn't have "sufficient rank" to be a guest at the mucky-muck table. He was the one who would later pull a .45 cal. on me in Tam Ky.

The Red Cross was there and one of them had wandered off. Somebody asked me to go find him, so I started heading north, where he could get into trouble. I was trying to figure out where a dumb-fuck, no-nothing pogue would go.

So I headed from the beach into the interior. I took a narrow trail. In the twilight I saw my boot take the slack out of a piece of fishing line stretched across the trail. I wheeled, ran and dove on to the beach as a huge ball of orange lit up the night. The beach shone bright for an instant and a patch of ocean in the foreground glowed. I rolled to my feet and turned back as I crouched, still backing up. Little globs of fire were scattered in the low brush. Willy Peter grenade. Mother-fucking white phosphorus. My brain jangled and I shuddered. A spectacular ball of fire in the night, and I didn't get touched. A split-second time delay in the firing mechanism and I'd escaped death again.

I took a few steps to where I flung my 16. I heard a motorbike and watched the headlight close in on me from up the beach. A Biet Lap rolled up with an American civilian on the back. Fucking Red Cross dipshit taking a tour. This was a close call I needed in the bank, not wasted on REMFs coming to the bush. Yeah, the ville was secure, but that trail I nearly bought it on was less than 200 meters from the outskirts of the ville. It wasn't all that far from where Keig stepped on the rigged 105 round and Cronin stepped on a toe-popper.

My disdain for REMFs was a two-way street. They didn't like me and I didn't want anything to do with them. I figured they didn't measure up. They had it dicked, and they resented my attitude, my independence. I was cut loose from the chain of command. We called the shots at 1-1-6. Looking back, I don't know why they would give a shit. They had their own little world and we had ours.

That staff sergeant at the celebration clearly had a case of the red ass over the small regard we had for the military in general. These were guys with eight or ten years in the corps and were likely making it their career. They had to dance to the tune of everybody that out-ranked them and probably had to kiss a lot of ass, put up with a lot of bullshit to get to the next rung on the ladder.

Meanwhile, we were out there acting like some kind of independent gang back on the block – a blight on their Marine Corps and a give-a-shit attitude they resented. This E-6 clearly hadn't been where I'd been and he clearly didn't have a clue about giving guys who were in the thick of it a little space.

I'm sitting on a cot in a small, low-sided, tin-roofed barracks in Marine detachment of an army MACV compound in Tam Ky. I'm waiting to catch a ride down Highway One to Chu Lai, that trip to headquarters to get reprimanded, or as a result of being ordered to see a shrink. I can't remember which. The barracks has a wood floor and the walls are lined with sandbags.

This E-6 is sitting on his cot. It must have been an NCO barracks or something. I don't know why I was waiting in there. I hear the incoming long before any others and judged it to be falling between the small airstrip and us. The round hit and the few guys in the hooch jumped up and ran for the door. The staff sergeant is the same guy that had his ass in a knot over me sitting at the table with

Vietnamese honchos at the celebration in Ky Phu Ville, where the Red Cross guy was thought to have wandered off on his own. Anyway, I don't budge. The rounds are short, obviously aimed at the landing strip where choppers are parked. The others jump up, charging for the door and the E-6 trips on the leg of a cot. Falls flat on his face in the middle of this cluster fuck of REMFs running for a bunker.

I'm still sitting there when they file back in after the four-or-so round barrage. The staff sergeant has a skinned nose from tripping over the leg of his cot.

"Well dude, looks like you're up for a Purple Heart," I said.

His face pinches up and his eyes glare as he strides up to me all in a huff.

"You will get your ass into a bunker when there is incoming. That's an order."

"Not if they're not even close, I'm not."

His face gets even redder. He unsnaps his holster and pulls out his .45 cal, and points it at my head.

My hand is on the grip of my .38 cal. Two guys are standing there open-mouthed. Numb nuts is standing over me with the safety on and probably no round in the chamber. I speak slowly.

"I will shoot you with this .38 before you can get the safety off and pull the slide back. You'd be dead by now, except I'd have to kill these two."

Chapter 50
Back in the World

Near the end of my tour, the investigation regarding the 13 killed NVA prisoners stalls my time to rotate home, and I'm called to the rear and assigned to teams in secure areas. I keep running into backstabbers from early days. Keep getting moved around from team to team, all of them in areas close to the rear and secure.

I keep running into assholes, thieves, racists from before, and I can't tolerate their presence. Justice is called for or something. Payback. I don't have to say jack and these guys know I want to fuck them up bad. A real chance with no witnesses – payback's a motherfucker. That's the code of the bush.

Their fear keeps getting me transferred until they bring me in to headquarters in Chu Lai. They want me to be a body guard for the first sergeant, but I tell him I'd sure as shit let somebody do him. Then I'm going to be the company commander's driver. He'd come on board recently. I drive him down Highway One to a CAP that took some mortar rounds or something. We are a "reaction force." He wants to get out of the rear.

I play chicken with other vehicles on the narrow road – one hand on the wheel, all nonchalant while nearly clipping mirrors of four-by-fours and deuce-and-a-halfs with the corner of the windshield. I drive like a maniac, but give plenty of room to people on bicycles or walking with the balance poles loaded down. I'd been told he doesn't want to slow down for anything, but he likes me, likes that

I'd spent my whole tour in the bush, been wounded and all that.

As I'm getting ready to rotate back to the world, he asks if I'd extend another three months; says he's heard about me. I stand in his office with a couple packets of telephone poles in one pocket and a big ball of opium rolled up in a pair of socks in the other.

He says, "Akins, this investigation will go nowhere if you extend another three months and be my driver."

"The only way I'll extend," I said, "is if I get jump school, sir."

Jumping out of planes sounds like fun.

"That's six months training," he says, "and you only have about six months left; they won't go for that."

When he realizes I won't extend, he goes to bat for me, gets the investigation dropped and gets me a flight home.

Thirteen months and a two-week hold-over. I'm relieved to get away but feel no cause for celebration. On the flight from Okinawa to the states I feel distraught, tense. My face feels hot and I sweat. Sweat about the next step. When I first landed in Da Nang a year plus earlier, I'd looked out the window, heaved a long sigh and wondered if I'd last 13 months. Now I fear stateside duty more than Viet Nam.

I'm certain of what lies ahead. I'd have to train troops. I have five months and 20 days left on my contract, and I can no longer skirt authority, and do things my way. I'd be an Infantry Training Regiment Instructor. No fucking way. I cannot be a part of a cannon-fodder production operation. I'd send new recruits to Mexico, to Canada. I'd end up in the brig, have to make up bad time, go AWOL –

the brig, then bad time. I'd never get out. I'd get trapped in a brig-bad-time Mobius Strip and never get out.

The flight to Okinawa feels awful; the flight to Travis worse. I cannot relax or feel any sense of relief. My stomach knots; I sweat on an air conditioned flight. I feel a deep sense of dread, worse than when I looked out of the airplane window 13 months ago when I landed at the same airstrip in Da Nang. I feel doomed.

I must have looked dangerous when we get off the bus at Treasure Island Naval Station. I must have had the 1000-yard stare of guys who had seen too much, done too much. I'm wearing the same faded camouflaged utilities and jungle boots that I came out of the bush with. I walk on the grass, don't salute.

Guy Yancy, a buddy from boot camp and infantry training recognizes me and stops up short. He'd spent most of his tour in Hawaii after getting his ass loaded with shrapnel. His eyes bug and his jaw drops.

"Akins. What the fuck happened to you?"

He keeps staring at me. Thirteen months roaming the dark night does something to you and your eyes, sunken features and menacing grin give it away. I'd startled myself looking into a mirror at the swift boat base in Chu Lai one night.

I get an early out. My Chinese buddy's efforts helped, but that visit to the shrink back in Chu Lai is probably the kiss of death for the rest of my obligation.

During that time I thought about my tour—how I'd survived, how I'd helped others make it. I daydreamed the welcome I'd receive, that I desired, even though I knew the anti-war sentiment was strong and gaining ground in 1969. I pictured a reporter and photographer from my hometown paper interviewing me when I get back to Tacoma, Washington.

When I call the airline to book a flight from Portland, Oregon to Tacoma Industrial Airport, the ticket agent is Kim Hamilton, from my neighborhood. She is the friend of mine to find out I was coming home. I didn't tell my parents I was back in the States, in Oregon. While I was in high school I'd carved Kim's and my initials in a tree along the lagoon at Titlow Park. She never knew I had a crush on her.

My mother picks me up at the small rural airstrip a few miles from home. It's just me and the pilot so I sit outside the entrance on a big rock in the sun. I watch her pull up into the empty gravel parking lot. I don't move, don't feel any desire to – just watch her eagerness and her glance at me without recognition as she sails right by.